EVERYONE**CAN**COOK
midweek meals

ERIC AKIS

EVERYONE**CAN**COOK
midweek meals

recipes for cooks on the run

whitecap

Whitecap Books

Whitecap Books is known for its expertise in the cookbook market and has produced some of the most innovative and familiar titles found in kitchens across North America.

Edited by Elaine Jones
Proofread by Lesley Cameron
Cover and interior design by Jacqui Thomas
Typesetting by Chrissy Davey
Food photography by Michael Tourigny
Author photo by Cheryl Warwick
Food styling by Eric Akis

Printed in Canada at Friesens.

LIBRARY AND ARCHIVES CANADA CATALOGUING IN PUBLICATION

Akis, Eric, 1961–
     Everyone can cook midweek meals / Eric Akis.

Includes index.
ISBN 978-1-55285-924-7

     1. Quick and easy cookery. I. Title.

TX833.5.A33 2008   641.5'55   C2007-905495-1

The publisher acknowledges the financial support of the Government of Canada through the Book Publishing Industry Development Program (BPIDP) and the province of British Columbia through the Book Publishing Tax Credit.

CONTENTS

EVERYONE**CAN**COOK
midweek meals

This book is dedicated to all the people who take the time, at least some of the time, no matter how busy they are, to prepare a tasty home-cooked, workday meal for their loved ones.

ACKNOWLEDGMENTS
This is the fourth book in my Everyone Can Cook series, and it has become evident over the years that I wouldn't have gotten as far as I have without the help of many people.

Thank you to absolutely everyone at Whitecap Books, particularly publisher Robert McCullough, for believing in me and being so supportive, and to editor Taryn Boyd, for so masterfully orchestrating the production of this book.

Thanks again to talented photographer Michael Tourigny (www.michaeltourigny.com) for taking, and helping to design, the wonderful photographs in this book, and to his assistant Laura Scotten for her fine post-production work.

Kudos to my friend Alison Field for, yet again, helping me with the metric conversions and the initial formatting of the recipes—you're a lifesaver, Ali!

To book editor Elaine Jones, thanks for helping me make the content of this book clearer and much richer.

To book designer Chrissy Davey, thank you for your inspired work. The book looks fabulous.

And last but not least, as always, my gratitude to my wife, Cheryl Warwick, and son, Tyler, for being at the table and enjoying all the midweek meals that made the creation of this book possible.

INTRODUCTION

Midweek meal preparation is one of the things that fall victim to the fast pace of modern life, where so many of us feel we have to rush, rush, rush. Putting a meal together is often seen as just another chore to quickly get out of the way when we're late for work or we've just finished a long workday or we're hungry and have activities to get to.

These are just some of the reasons why we often feel the need to hurriedly plunk a meal on the table, and marketers of factory-prepared, ready-to-heat foods have done a masterful job of playing it up. I've lost count of the TV commercials I've seen that picture a stressed-out parent's smiling family digging into a dish that came in a shiny box and took only minutes to prepare—that is, heat up.

These products are certainly convenient, but relying on them means you and your family and guests will regularly be eating foods that often contain a long list of hard-to-pronounce ingredients to make them shelf stable. More importantly, it instills the notion in younger people that instant meals are what people normally eat. In fact, when you do take the time to cook something from scratch, they may turn up their noses at it because you won't be using the large amount of salt and artificial flavorings that make processed food so addictively intense.

Whenever I get the chance, I try to change the belief that preparing a midweek meal is a horrible task; instead, it's a pleasurable way to relax and put memories of a busy day behind you. In fact, the aroma of fresh-chopped garlic sautéing in a pan for a homemade pasta dish, the beautiful colors of vegetables especially picked for a stir-fry or the rich taste of glazed and baked salmon can become as addictive as the boxed foods!

I'm betting most home cooks will find this extra effort worth it, particularly if they choose user-friendly recipes for quickly getting delicious meals on the table. That's where I come in.

Everyone Can Cook Midweek Meals offers breakfast, lunch, dinner and dessert recipes to suit a range of palates—from traditional family fare to slow cooker meals to tastes from around the world. When designing the recipes, I kept two things in mind.

The first was to create dishes that can be quickly whipped up, such as Baked Fish with Sweet Chili Citrus Glaze (page 133), Kebabs in a Pita (page 143) or Tortellini Alfredo (page 80). The second was to offer an assortment of recipes that you can make ahead, perhaps on a day off. These can be stored in the refrigerator or freezer and quickly cooked, reheated, or simply thawed when needed. Examples include Bake and Freeze Pumpkin Date Muffins (page 11), Quick and Easy Vegetable and Pasta Soup (page 24) and Large Batch Roast and Freeze Meatballs (page 159).

The recipes here, like those in the first three books of the series, are also intended to appeal to all levels of cooks and focus on using accessible ingredients. For each recipe, Eric's Options offers suggestions for substituting, adding or omitting an ingredient if desired. The section on stocking the pantry provides a list of basic ingredients to have on hand, and cooking tips scattered through the book will further guide cooks on how to make a home-cooked meal an undemanding and joyous experience.

My belief is that with *Everyone Can Cook Midweek Meals* on their kitchen bookshelf, home cooks on the run will want to run home and cook!

STOCKING
YOUR PANTRY

Midweek meal preparation is a much quicker proposition if you're not running to the grocery store after work to pick up kitchen staples. Having key ingredients on hand can also aid a spur of the moment decision to make baked goods, such as a batch of cookies. Following are some of the important items to have on hand in your cupboards, refrigerator and freezer. With these at the ready, preparing the delicious recipes in this book will be fun, fast and easy.

ASIAN SAUCES, NOODLES AND OTHER STAPLES

North Americans are fond of Asian-style dishes and there are a number of recipes in this book. Soy sauce, teriyaki sauce, sweet chili sauce, hot chili sauce, coconut milk, mini-corn and hoisin sauce are items you should stock. Alongside them should be quick-cooking Asian-style noodles, such as the egg, rice and udon noodles used in this book. Noodle package sizes vary; if you can't find the exact size called for in a recipe, use what you need from the package and save the rest for another time.

BAKING BASICS

If you have time and the urge to bake something on a midweek evening, fulfilling that desire will be easier if you keep some basic ingredients on hand. Key items include all-purpose flour, whole wheat flour, rolled oats, granulated sugar, icing sugar, brown sugar, baking powder, baking soda, pure vanilla extract, butter, eggs, vegetable shortening, cocoa powder and chocolate chips.

BREADCRUMBS

Keep a bag of breadcrumbs on hand to coat foods before pan-frying or baking and to add body to meatball and burger mixes.

CANNED FISH

Keep tins of tuna and salmon on your shelf and you'll have an instant, protein-rich ingredient to use in sandwiches, salads and other tasty creations.

CANNED LEGUMES

Chickpeas, white and/or red kidney beans and black beans are three tinned legumes that form the basis of a variety of recipes in this book, including soup, burgers and stew.

CANNED TOMATO PRODUCTS

Diced and whole tomatoes, tomato sauce, pasta sauce and tomato paste, which you can also buy in a tube, are important items to keep on hand to make chili and Italian-style dishes.

CHEESE AND OTHER DAIRY PRODUCTS

A little cheese can add a lot of flavor. Mozzarella, goat, feta, cheddar, Monterey Jack and Parmesan are versatile cheeses I like to keep in the refrigerator. Yogurt, sour cream, whipping cream and, of course, milk are other dairy products used in this book to make or top dishes such as eggs, noodle dishes and baked goods.

CURRY PASTES AND POWDER

These are two splendid Asian-style ingredients that come in mild, medium and hot versions. They're used in this book to add life to a sandwich filling, spice up roast chicken and flavor a vegetarian stew.

DIJON MUSTARD

I buy this versatile ingredient in a large jar because it's useful in all sorts of recipes, including salad dressings, sauces, braised dishes and roasts.

DRIED HERBS AND SPICES

Everyone has a drawer full of these, but here are the basics for recipes in this book: thyme, tarragon, ground and crumbled sage, herbes de Provence, rosemary, paprika, chili powder, ground cumin, ground cinnamon, ground nutmeg, ground cloves and five-spice powder.

FRESH PRODUCE

All refrigerators contain some fresh produce, but items making several appearances in this book include garlic, ginger, yellow (Spanish) onions, green onions, celery, carrots, mini-carrots, bell peppers, new potatoes, Yukon Gold potatoes, baking potatoes, snap peas, snow peas, leaf lettuce, organic mixed salad greens, tomatoes, apples, lemons, limes and oranges.

FROZEN PEAS AND CORN

Use these little frozen gems to add color, texture and taste to a range of dishes, such as chili, stews and soups.

HONEY AND MAPLE SYRUP

Beyond adding sweetness, these ingredients are also used to balance tart, spicy flavorings in salad dressings, sauces and bastes.

MAYONNAISE

Many people think of mayonnaise as simply a sandwich spread or salad binder, but it also makes a base for quick salad dressings and can be used to coat foods, such as fish fillets, before breading.

NUTS AND DRIED FRUIT

Keep walnuts, pecans, almonds, raisins, dried cranberries, currants and other nuts and dried fruit on hand to use in granola, salads and desserts. (See How to Store Nuts, page 40, and Storing Dried Fruit, page 42.)

OILS

It's hard to imagine cooking without oils, which contribute moisture and flavor to a range of dishes, from salads to stir-fries, meats, seafood and baked goods. The two main types I stock are extra virgin olive oil, which I use to prepare Mediterranean-style dishes, and vegetable oil, which has a high smoking point and is ideal for high-temperature searing of foods and stir-frying.

PASTA

If you're looking for a quick supper, a bag of dried pasta in your cupboard or a package of fresh pasta in your refrigerator will be the answer. Cook it up, toss it with a tasty sauce or other flavorful ingredients, and voila, dinner is ready. Stock various shapes and sizes, such as spaghetti, linguini, macaroni, rotini, penne, rigatoni and tortellini.

PESTO

This delicious ingredient appears several times in this book, adding color and flavor to an assortment of dishes. Almost every supermarket sells prepared pesto that will keep a week or more in your refrigerator. You can also make homemade pesto and freeze it in cubes (see About Pesto, page 31).

PREPARED STOCKS

Some very good prepared vegetable, chicken and beef stocks are available in supermarkets these days. Have them on hand to make soups, stews or braised dishes.

TORTILLAS AND OTHER FLATBREADS

Flour tortillas are handy and versatile: stuff and roll them to make wraps, add pizza toppings and bake them, tear them into chunks and dunk them in soup. Other flatbreads to keep on hand include pita (both flat and with pockets) and naan bread.

VINEGAR

Stock balsamic, cider, rice and wine vinegars to flavor salad dressings and other dishes that benefit from an acidic bite.

BRILLIANT BREAKFASTS

CHAPTER ONE

SPICED GRAPEFRUIT BRÛLÉE

preparation time · 5 minutes
cooking time · 2 minutes
makes · 2 servings

Brûlée is a French cooking technique where a topping of sugar is caramelized under a broiler or with a blowtorch—this is often done with a cup of custard, as in crème brûlée. In this breakfast treat, tangy, nutritious grapefruit is deliciously sweetened with spiced-up, golden brown sugar.

ERIC'S OPTIONS
To speed up preparation at breakfast time, combine the sugar and spices and halve and segment the grapefruit the night before.

1	large grapefruit, sliced in half	1
2 Tbsp	packed golden brown sugar	30 mL
pinch each	cinnamon, nutmeg and cloves	pinch each

Set the oven rack 6 inches (15 cm) beneath the broiler. Preheat the broiler. Cut between the segments of the fruit with a grapefruit knife so the flesh will be easier to scoop out after broiling. Place the grapefruit, cut-side up, in a small baking dish. Combine the brown sugar and spices in a small bowl; sprinkle the mixture on top of the grapefruit. Broil the grapefruit for 2 minutes, or until the sugar is bubbly and caramelized.

ABOUT GRAPEFRUIT

When buying grapefruits, choose smooth ones with brightly colored skin. The best grapefruits will feel heavy for their size—an indication they're packed with juice. Grapefruit can be stored for a few days at room temperature. If you've bought a big bag and need to keep them longer, store them in the crisper of your refrigerator for up to 2 weeks. Remove and leave at room temperature overnight for juicier fruit. Grapefruit is low in calories and rich in vitamin C. It also contains folic acid and potassium and is a good source of inositol, a member of the vitamin B complex, which studies have shown may help lower blood cholesterol levels.

YOU-CHOOSE-THE-FRUIT SMOOTHIES

preparation time · 5 minutes
cooking time · none
makes · 2 generous servings

Flavor this energy-filled breakfast smoothie with your favorite fruit or whatever you have on hand. Kiwis, mangoes, bananas, melons, berries or a mixture are all good choices.

ERIC'S OPTIONS
For a richer-tasting smoothie, use full-fat instead of low-fat yogurt. Substitute any other type of juice, such as pineapple or cranberry, for orange juice, and try using maple syrup as a sweetener instead of honey.

2 cups	sliced or cubed fresh fruit	500 mL
1 cup	low-fat yogurt	250 mL
¼ cup	orange juice	60 mL
1 tsp	freshly grated ginger	5 mL
2 tsp	honey, or to taste	10 mL
	sliced or whole fresh fruit for garnish (optional)	

Place the 2 cups (500 mL) of fruit, yogurt, orange juice, ginger and honey in a food processor or blender. Pulse until smooth. Pour into glasses, garnish with sliced or whole fruit, if desired, and serve.

HOMEMADE HOT CHOCOLATE MIX

preparation time · 10 minutes
cooking time · none
makes · 4 cups (1 L) (enough for 12–16 mugs of hot chocolate)

If your kids or you like to wake up with a mug of hot chocolate, this recipe is for you. It's easy to make and you get to control the ingredients that go into it.

ERIC'S OPTIONS
Double the recipe if your house is filled with hot-chocolate fanatics. For sweet and spicy hot chocolate, add ¼–½ tsp (1–2 mL) of ground cayenne pepper to the mix when stirring in the skim milk powder.

1½ cups	icing sugar	375 mL
¾ cup	cocoa powder	175 mL
1 tsp	ground cinnamon	5 mL
1½ cups	skim milk powder	375 mL
2 cups	mini-marshmallows (optional)	500 mL

Sift the icing sugar, cocoa and cinnamon into a large bowl. Thoroughly whisk in the skim milk powder. Stir in the mini-marshmallows, if using. Store in an airtight container at cool room temperature; the mix will keep for several weeks.

To make a serving of hot chocolate, spoon ¼ cup (60 mL) to ⅓ cup (75 mL) of the mix into a mug. Add 1 cup (250 mL) of hot water or milk, stir to combine and serve.

MAPLE CRUNCH GRANOLA

preparation time · 15 minutes
cooking time · 25–30 minutes
makes · about 12 servings, ½ cup (125 mL) each

Make this nutritious mixture of oats, fruit, nuts and seeds on your day off and you'll have 12 delicious breakfast servings or snacks you can pack for work or school in a bag. Purchase large flake rolled oats, not the quick-cooking kind.

ERIC'S OPTIONS

This recipe can be doubled. If desired, substitute other dried fruits, such as blueberries and cherries, and other unsalted nuts, such as walnuts or cashews, for some of those called for in the recipe. Substitute an equal amount of honey for the maple syrup.

3 cups	large flake rolled oats	750 mL
¼ cup	dried cranberries	60 mL
¼ cup	raisins or currants	60 mL
¼ cup	slivered almonds	60 mL
¼ cup	sunflower seeds	60 mL
¼ cup	pecan halves, coarsely chopped	60 mL
¼ cup	pumpkin seeds	60 mL
¼ cup	unsweetened coconut flakes	60 mL
12	dried apricots, sliced	12
½ tsp	ground cinnamon	2 mL
½ cup	maple syrup	125 mL
¼ cup	vegetable oil	60 mL

Instructions follow on page 9 ...

MAPLE CRUNCH
GRANOLA (CONTINUED)

Preheat the oven to 325°F (160°C). Line an 11- x 17-inch (28 x 43 cm) or similar-sized baking sheet with parchment paper. Place the oats, cranberries, raisins or currants, almonds, sunflower seeds, pecans, pumpkin seeds, coconut, apricots and cinnamon in a large bowl and toss to combine.

Combine the maple syrup and oil in a small pot. Set over medium heat until warm, but not hot. Pour into the bowl with the dry ingredients and stir well. Spread the mixture on the prepared baking sheet. Bake for 25–30 minutes, stirring 2 or 3 times, until the oats and other ingredients are lightly toasted. Cool on a rack to room temperature.

Transfer to an airtight container and store at cool room temperature for up to 3 weeks.

To serve, scoop ½ cup (125 mL) of the granola into a bowl and top with milk, soy beverage or yogurt.

WHY EAT OATS?

If you're looking for a nutritious food, look no further. Oats are low in fat, an excellent source of thiamine and B vitamins and a good source of iron, potassium and other minerals—and they contain vitamin E. They're rich in soluble fiber, believed to help reduce blood cholesterol levels. The bran surrounding the oat kernel is much thinner and paler than other grains, such as wheat. It is not removed during milling, and so retains all its nutritional value.

YOGURT, BERRY and GRANOLA PARFAIT

preparation time · 5 minutes
cooking time · none
makes · 2 servings

A parfait is basically several delicious foods layered in a tall glass—in this case tangy yogurt, colorful berries and crunchy granola. Not only is it beautiful, it's also healthy! Use any berries you like, such as strawberries, blueberries or raspberries.

ERIC'S OPTIONS
Use store-bought granola if you haven't made your own. If you don't care for vanilla-flavored yogurt, substitute plain or fruit-flavored yogurt. For a tropical-tasting parfait, replace the berries with a mix of sliced or cubed mango, pineapple and banana.

1 cup	Maple Crunch Granola (see page 7) plus a sprinkle for garnish	250 mL
1½ cups	mixed fresh berries	375 mL
1½ cups	vanilla-flavored yogurt	375 mL

Divide the granola evenly between 2 wine glasses or other tall glasses. Top each with ½ cup (125 mL) of the berries and spoon the yogurt overtop. Finish with the remaining fruit and garnish the tops with a little more granola. Serve immediately.

BAKE and FREEZE PUMPKIN DATE MUFFINS

preparation time ·	25–30 minutes	
cooking time ·	18–20 minutes	
makes ·	24 medium-sized muffins	

These nutritious and delicious muffins freeze beautifully, making them perfect for a large batch. Enjoy some fresh and freeze the rest to warm for a quick midweek breakfast.

ERIC'S OPTIONS
This recipe can be halved. Instead of dates, use another type of dried fruit, such as cranberries or raisins. For a decorative touch, sprinkle the muffins with pumpkin seeds before baking. Instead of muffins, make this recipe into two 9- x 5-inch (2 L) loaves—great to serve at teatime or for dessert. The loaves will take 50 minutes to bake; baking temperature remains the same. Cool before slicing.

4	large eggs	4
1½ cups	packed golden brown sugar	375 mL
1	14 oz (398 mL) can pumpkin	1
1½ cups	unsweetened applesauce	375 mL
2 tsp	pure vanilla extract	10 mL
2 cups	whole wheat flour	500 mL
1 cup	all-purpose flour	250 mL
2 tsp	ground cinnamon	10 mL
1 tsp	ground ginger	5 mL
2 tsp	baking soda	10 mL
2 tsp	baking powder	10 mL
1 tsp	salt	5 mL
1 cup	chopped dates	250 mL
1 cup	chopped walnuts or pecan pieces	250 mL
	vegetable oil spray	

Instructions follow on page 13 ...

BAKE and FREEZE PUMPKIN DATE MUFFINS (CONTINUED)

Preheat the oven to 375°F (190°C). Whisk the eggs, brown sugar, pumpkin, applesauce and vanilla in a large bowl until the mixture is smooth. In a second bowl, mix together the whole wheat and all-purpose flours with the cinnamon, ginger, baking soda, baking powder and salt using a whisk. Stir the dates and nuts into the dry mixture. Add the dry ingredients to the wet and mix until just combined.

Spray two 12-cup nonstick muffin pans lightly with vegetable oil. Spoon the batter evenly into the cups. Bake the muffins for 18–20 minutes. Cool in the pans for 15 minutes. Carefully remove the muffins from the pan (and enjoy some while they're still warm). Freeze leftover muffins in an airtight container after they have cooled to room temperature. To reheat, thaw at room temperature overnight and then warm for a few minutes in a 200°F (95°C) oven.

PREPARING YOUR OWN PUMPKIN

Canned puréed pumpkin is a great timesaver, but you may want to try making your own in the fall, when fresh pumpkins are inexpensive. Split the pumpkin in half and remove the seeds and stringy bits. Place the pumpkin halves, shell-side up, in a roasting pan lined with parchment paper. Bake in a 325°F (160°C) oven until it's very tender and the sides of the pumpkin start to collapse, about 1 hour. Cool to room temperature and then scrape the flesh off the skin. Pulse the flesh in a food processor until smooth. The resulting purée, which can be frozen for later use, can be used in pies, loaves, cookies, muffins and soup.

EGG and SAUSAGE–STUFFED ENGLISH MUFFINS

preparation time · 10 minutes
cooking time · 2–3 minutes
makes · 2 servings

Use a stainless egg ring to create a perfectly round egg for these muffins. You can buy them at most stores that sell kitchenware.

ERIC'S OPTIONS
Instead of an English muffin, use a crusty roll, homemade biscuit or scone. If you don't have an egg ring, simply fry the eggs in a skillet as you normally would.

2 tsp	vegetable oil, plus some for the egg rings	10 mL
2	large eggs	2
2	white or whole wheat English muffins, split	2
	butter, at room temperature (optional)	
2	Pork and Oat Patties, heated through (see page 17)	2
2	thin slices aged cheddar cheese	2

Heat the oil in a nonstick skillet over medium heat. Lightly oil 2 egg rings, set them in the skillet and crack an egg into each ring. Break the yolk, if desired. Cover the pan and cook the eggs until they're just set, about 2–3 minutes. While the eggs cook, toast the English muffins and lightly butter, if desired. When the eggs are ready, place 1 on the bottom half of each muffin, add a pork and oat patty and a slice of cheese and finish with the muffin top. Serve immediately.

EGGS: THE WONDER FOOD

When I was younger and had little money, I always had eggs on hand to see me through. Inexpensive, easy to prepare, relatively low in calories and very nutritious, they provide high-quality protein, every vitamin except C and minerals such as iron. Some people think brown eggs are superior to white when it comes to nutritional content, but the values are the same.

When preparing eggs, whether by frying, poaching or boiling, don't crank up the heat and rush things. If you cook them in gently simmering water or over medium heat, you'll improve your chances of getting perfectly cooked, tender eggs, not overcooked, rubbery ones.

Check the best-before date before buying eggs and store them in the refrigerator; eggs kept at room temperature lose their quality quickly. Believe it or not, eggshells are porous and the flavor of an egg can be affected if exposed to odorous foods in your refrigerator. Unless your refrigerator has a separate, closed area to store eggs, keep them in the carton you bought them in. It was designed to protect the eggs and maximize their shelf life.

ENGLISH MUFFIN
BLTs

preparation time · 10 minutes
cooking time · 4–5 minutes
makes · 2 servings

Lean Canadian bacon—also called back bacon—is cured, sliced and fully cooked pork loin that just needs to be heated through before serving, which makes this breakfast sandwich a snap to make.

ERIC'S OPTIONS
If time allows, fry up 2–4 slices of regular strip bacon instead of Canadian bacon. For a more filling sandwich, add a fried egg.

1 tsp	vegetable oil	5 mL
2–4	slices Canadian bacon	2–4
2	white or whole wheat English muffins, split	2
to taste	mayonnaise	to taste
2	leaves lettuce	2
6	slices ripe tomato	6

Place the oil in a nonstick skillet and set over medium heat. Add the bacon and cook for 2 minutes per side, or until heated through. While the bacon cooks, toast the English muffins and spread with mayonnaise. Place a lettuce leaf on the bottom half of each muffin and top with the tomatoes and bacon. Replace the top and serve immediately.

PORK and OAT PATTIES

preparation time	·	15 minutes
cooking time	·	4–6 minutes
makes	·	8 patties

These tasty homemade patties can be formed, cooked, individually wrapped, frozen and reheated when you need them. To reheat, place the frozen patties in a nonstick skillet over medium-low to medium heat. Cover and cook until thawed and heated through, about 5 minutes.

ERIC'S OPTIONS

For different textures, substitute an equal amount of bread or cornflake crumbs for the oats. For added color, mix 1 Tbsp (15 mL) of chopped fresh parsley into the pork mixture before forming into patties. Or use other fresh herbs, such as rosemary or thyme.

1 lb	lean ground pork	500 g
¼ cup	quick-cooking rolled oats	60 mL
1	large egg, beaten	1
½ tsp	dried crumbled sage	2 mL
¼ tsp	paprika	1 mL
½ tsp	salt	2 mL
½ tsp	freshly ground black pepper	2 mL
2 Tbsp	vegetable oil	30 mL

Place the pork, oats, egg, sage, paprika, salt and pepper in a bowl and gently mix to combine. Moisten your hands with cold water to help prevent sticking and divide the mixture into 8 balls. Shape each ball into a ¼-inch-thick (6 mm) patty.

Heat the oil in a large skillet over medium heat. Cook the patties 2–3 minutes per side, or until entirely cooked through.

WHOLE WHEAT
BREAKFAST BURRITOS

preparation time · 10 minutes
cooking time · 3–4 minutes
makes · 4 servings

This breakfast, Tex-Mex style, is one all ages will enjoy.

ERIC'S OPTIONS
Substitute plain or flavored tortillas, such as spinach or jalapeño, for the whole wheat. Give the burritos a meaty taste by adding 1 or 2 chorizo sausages, cooked and sliced, to the egg mixture before scrambling.

4	10-inch (25 cm) whole wheat tortilla shells	4
6	large eggs, beaten	6
¼ cup	milk	60 mL
to taste	salt and freshly ground black pepper	to taste
2 Tbsp	vegetable oil	30 mL
1 cup	grated Monterey Jack, mozzarella or cheddar cheese	250 mL
⅓–½ cup	tomato salsa	75–125 mL
1 cup	shredded leaf or head lettuce	250 mL

Preheat the oven to 350°F (180°C). Stack the tortillas, wrap in foil and warm in the oven for 5 minutes. While the tortillas warm, combine the eggs, milk, salt and pepper in a bowl. Heat the oil in a large, nonstick skillet over medium heat. Add the eggs; cook and stir until just cooked through. Place the eggs in a row along the center of each warmed tortilla. Arrange the cheese, salsa and lettuce alongside the eggs, dividing them equally between the tortillas. Fold the sides of each tortilla over and tightly roll into a closed cylinder. Serve immediately.

ONE-PAN FAMILY BREAKFAST

preparation time · 20 minutes
cooking time · 6–8 minutes
makes · 4 servings

Make extra boiled potatoes for dinner and save a couple to make this the next morning. It's a quick way to cook a substantial breakfast for a family of 4.

ERIC'S OPTIONS
Halve the recipe if you're serving 2. If you like mushrooms, clean and slice 6 and add them to the skillet with the ham, potatoes and bell pepper. For a vegetarian version, omit the ham and add a cupful (250mL) of another vegetable, such as diced zucchini.

2 Tbsp	butter	30 mL
1 cup	cubed ham	250 mL
2	medium red potatoes, boiled until tender, cooled and cubed	2
¼ cup	finely chopped red bell pepper	60 mL
8	large eggs	8
¼ cup	milk or water	60 mL
1 cup	grated cheddar cheese	250 mL
2	green onions, finely chopped	2
to taste	salt and freshly ground black pepper	to taste

Melt the butter in a large nonstick skillet over medium-high heat. Add the ham, potatoes and bell pepper and cook for 3 or 4 minutes, stirring occasionally. Whisk the eggs with the milk until well combined. Stir the cheese, green onions, salt and pepper into the egg mixture and pour into the pan. As the eggs begin to set, gently turn and lift them from the bottom and sides of the skillet, forming large, soft curds. When the eggs are just set, divide among 4 plates and serve immediately with toast.

BAKED FRENCH TOAST
with CINNAMON

preparation time · 20 minutes
cooking time · 27–28 minutes
makes · 4 servings (2 slices each)

Serve this to your kids when they have an active day planned at school and you want to make sure they're off to a good start. The preparation can be done the night before; the next morning you can serve a hot breakfast in less than 30 minutes.

ERIC'S OPTIONS

Make the French toast spicier and even more aromatic by mixing pinches of ground nutmeg and cloves into the brown sugar along with the cinnamon. For fruit-filled French toast, use thick slices of raisin bread instead of French bread. For more fiber, use thick slices of whole wheat bread.

3 Tbsp	butter, melted	45 mL
½ cup	packed golden brown sugar	125 mL
½ tsp	ground cinnamon	2 mL
8	1-inch-thick (2.5 cm) slices French bread	8
4	large eggs	4
½ cup	milk	125 mL
½ cup	light (10%) cream	125 mL
¼ cup	orange juice	60 mL

Coat a 9- x 13-inch (3.5 L) baking pan with the melted butter. Combine the sugar and cinnamon in a small bowl and sprinkle half of it evenly into the bottom of the pan. Place the bread slices in a single layer in the pan, squeezing them in to make them fit if necessary.

Beat the eggs in a medium bowl until the yolks and whites are thoroughly combined. Mix in the milk, cream and orange juice. Slowly pour this mixture over the bread, ensuring each slice is evenly coated. Sprinkle the top of the bread with the remaining brown sugar mixture. Cover and refrigerate overnight.

The next morning, place the rack in the middle position and preheat the oven to 375°F (190°C). Uncover the dish and bake the French toast for 25 minutes. Turn the oven to broil and broil the French toast for 2–3 minutes, or until the top is golden brown. Serve with warm maple syrup.

SKILLET BREAKFAST
for ONE

preparation time · 5 minutes
cooking time · 5–6 minutes
makes · 1 serving

This hearty breakfast is ready in minutes and will sustain you all morning. Serve it with toast or a warm scone or croissant.

ERIC'S OPTIONS
Add 1 or 2 tsp (5 or 10 mL) of chopped parsley, chives or dill to the egg mixture before scrambling the eggs. If you're a fan of blue cheese, crumble a little on top of the eggs just before serving.

2	large eggs, beaten	2
1 Tbsp	milk or water	15 mL
to taste	salt and freshly ground black pepper	to taste
pinch	cayenne pepper	pinch
2 tsp	vegetable oil	10 mL
2–3	thin slices Black Forest or country-style ham	2–3
3	thick slices tomato	3

Whisk the eggs, milk, salt, pepper and cayenne in a bowl until well mixed. Heat the oil in a small, nonstick skillet over medium-high heat. Add the ham and cook for 1–2 minutes, or until heated through. Transfer the ham to a heated plate.

Add the tomatoes to the skillet and cook for about 30 seconds per side; remove and place on top of the ham. Add the eggs to the skillet and cook, stirring with a wooden spoon to scramble them. Spoon the eggs on top of the tomatoes and ham; serve immediately.

LUNCH TO GO

CHAPTER TWO

QUICK and EASY VEGETABLE and PASTA SOUP

preparation time	·	5 minutes
cooking time	·	10 minutes
makes	·	2 servings

Make this soup in just a few minutes and serve it with a crusty whole wheat roll for a hearty lunch.

ERIC'S OPTIONS
If you have some cooked meat on hand, such as beef or chicken, chop and add ⅓ cup (75 mL) to the soup when bringing the other ingredients to a simmer. Instead of pasta, use ⅓ cup (75 mL) canned legumes, such as chickpeas or white kidney beans.

2–3	green beans, chopped	2–3
¼ cup	diced carrot	60 mL
1	medium ripe tomato, chopped	1
¼ cup	macaroni or other small pasta	60 mL
1¾ cups	chicken, beef or vegetable stock	425 mL
pinch each	dried oregano and basil	pinch each
¼ cup	frozen corn kernels	60 mL
1	green onion, finely chopped	1
to taste	salt and freshly ground black pepper	to taste

Place the beans, carrot, tomato, pasta, stock, oregano and basil in a small soup pot. Bring to a boil, and then reduce the heat to a gentle simmer. Simmer for 6–8 minutes, or until the pasta and vegetables are tender. Mix in the corn, green onion, salt and pepper. Remove from the heat and cool the soup to room temperature. Refrigerate until ready to reheat for lunch.

TOMATO and OLIVE BRUSCHETTA TO GO

preparation time	·	10 minutes
cooking time	·	8–10 minutes
makes	·	1 serving

A satisfying, Italian-style lunch rich in vitamin C.

ERIC'S OPTIONS
For added protein, top the bruschetta with a few paper-thin slices of Italian-style meat, such as salami or capicola. Instead of Italian bread, make the bruschetta with another type of loaf, such as French, olive or sourdough.

1	thick slice Italian bread, cut in half	1
2 Tbsp	extra virgin olive oil	30 mL
1 Tbsp	freshly grated Parmesan cheese	15 mL
1	medium to large ripe tomato, chopped	1
2 tsp	homemade or store-bought pesto (see About Pesto, page 31)	10 mL
4–6	pitted green or black olives, sliced	4–6
to taste	salt and freshly ground black pepper	to taste

Preheat the oven (a toaster oven if you have one) to 400°F (200°C). Brush 1 side of the bread pieces lightly with ½ Tbsp (7.5 mL) of the olive oil. Set them on a small baking sheet and sprinkle with the Parmesan cheese. Bake for 8–10 minutes, or until lightly toasted. Cool, place in a takeout container or bag and store at room temperature. Combine the remaining 1½ Tbsp (22.5 mL) olive oil, tomato, pesto, olives, salt and pepper. in a takeout container; cover and store in the refrigerator until lunchtime. To serve, top each piece of bread with an equal amount of tomato mixture and enjoy.

CURRIED SHRIMP–STUFFED PAPAYA

preparation time · 5 minutes
cooking time · none
makes · 1 serving

This may sound a bit decadent for lunch, but it costs about the same as a fast food burger meal and is much more nutritious. It also tastes simply divine.

ERIC'S OPTIONS
If you're in a hurry, don't worry about the curry, mayonnaise and other ingredients, just place the shrimp in the cavity of the papaya along with the lime wedges. Simple but also delicious!

½ cup	cooked salad shrimp, patted dry	125 mL
1–2 Tbsp	mayonnaise	15–30 mL
¼ tsp	curry powder	1 mL
1 Tbsp	finely chopped red bell pepper	15 mL
1 Tbsp	finely chopped celery	15 mL
1	green onion, finely chopped	1
to taste	salt	to taste
½	small to medium ripe papaya, seeds removed	½
2	lime wedges	2

Place the shrimp, mayonnaise, curry powder, bell pepper, celery, green onion and salt in a bowl and mix to combine. Fill the cavity of the papaya with the shrimp mixture. Place the lime wedges on top, wrap and chill until lunchtime. Squeeze the lime over the shrimp just before eating.

ABOUT SALAD SHRIMP

Small, cooked salad shrimp are available at most supermarkets and seafood stores. They are sold fresh, frozen or thawed from frozen, something retailers will do so customers can use them right away. If you've bought them fresh or thawed from frozen, remember that they're highly perishable. It's best to buy them the day you need them, but they could be stored up to 1 day in the coldest part of your refrigerator. If you've bought frozen shrimp, the safest way to maintain quality and thaw them is in the refrigerator overnight. Pat them dry with a paper towel before using them, as any liquid can dilute or negatively affect the taste of the dish you're making.

Teriyaki Soba Noodle and Vegetable Salad (facing page) and Pasta Salad with Broccoli, Tomatoes and Pesto (page 30)

TERIYAKI SOBA NOODLE
and VEGETABLE SALAD

preparation time · 10 minutes
cooking time · 5 minutes
makes · 1 serving

Soba noodles are a Japanese-style noodle made with earthy-tasting buckwheat flour. They're sold at Asian markets and most supermarkets. Make this salad the night before and its flavors will meld deliciously by the time you're ready for lunch.

ERIC'S OPTIONS
Use another type of Asian noodle, such as rice or egg noodle. Substitute your favorite vegetables or those you may have on hand, such as small broccoli florets, chopped yellow bell pepper, sliced snap peas or thickly grated English cucumber. This recipe can be doubled.

3 oz	soba noodles (see Note)	75 g
3 Tbsp	teriyaki sauce	45 mL
¼ tsp	hot Asian-style chili sauce, or to taste	1 mL
1 tsp	vegetable oil	5 mL
⅓ cup	grated carrot	75 mL
⅓ cup	chopped red bell pepper	75 mL
8	snow peas, trimmed and thickly sliced	8
1	green onion, finely chopped	1

Cook the noodles in a generous amount of boiling water until just tender, about 5 minutes. While the noodles cook, combine the remaining ingredients in a medium bowl. When the noodles are cooked, drain them well, cool in ice-cold water and drain well again. Add them to the bowl and toss to combine; cover and chill until ready to eat.

NOTE
Soba noodles come in a range of package sizes, depending on the producer. I used a little less than a third of a 10 oz (about 275 g) package to get the amount required for this recipe.

PASTA SALAD with BROCCOLI, TOMATOES and PESTO

preparation time	·	15 minutes
cooking time	·	7–8 minutes
makes	·	2 servings

Twirly pasta and fresh vegetables look pretty and make a lively tasting, healthy and substantial lunch.

ERIC'S OPTIONS
If you like mayonnaise-based pasta salads, omit the oil from this recipe and mix in 2–3 Tbsp (30–45 mL) of mayonnaise. Instead of cherry tomatoes, use 1 large, ripe tomato, diced.

1½ cups	rotini or other bite-sized pasta	375 mL
2–3 Tbsp	homemade or store-bought pesto (see About Pesto, page 31)	30–45 mL
1 Tbsp	extra virgin olive oil	15 mL
to taste	salt and freshly ground black pepper	to taste
2–3 Tbsp	freshly grated Parmesan cheese	30–45 mL
12–14	small broccoli florets, blanched (see How to Blanch Vegetables, page 32)	12–14
8	cherry tomatoes, halved	8
⅓ cup	grated carrot	75 mL
2	lemon wedges	2

Bring a large pot of lightly salted water to a boil. Add the pasta and cook until just tender, about 7–8 minutes. Drain well, cool in ice-cold water, drain well again and place in a medium bowl. Add the pesto, oil, salt, pepper and cheese; toss to coat the rotini. Add the broccoli, tomatoes and carrot and gently toss to combine. Refrigerate the salad.

Gently toss the salad again before packing it and the lemon wedges into 2 takeout containers with tight-fitting lids. Squeeze the lemon overtop just before serving the salad.

ABOUT PESTO

All supermarkets sell good-quality prepared pesto these days. I use it to flavor all sorts of dishes, from soups to pasta to grilled sandwiches. In the summer, though, when basil is abundant and cheap at farmers' markets, I like to make my own pesto.

Pesto, which originated in Genoa, Italy, takes its name from the Italian word *pestare*, which means to pound or crush. Traditionally, a mortar and pestle were used to pound the uncooked ingredients into a sauce. For a midweek meal, pounding your own pesto would be too time-consuming, but it's not difficult to make a batch in a food processor on a day off so it will be ready during the week when you need it.

To make pesto, place 4 cups (1 L) basil leaves, packed, in a food processor with 3–4 sliced garlic cloves, ½ cup (125 mL) pine nuts and ½ cup (125 mL) freshly grated Parmesan cheese (optional). Pulse until coarsely chopped. Slowly add ¾–1 cup (175–250 mL) extra virgin olive oil and process until smooth. If you find the pesto too thick, add a little more oil. Makes about 1½ cups (375 mL).

Refrigerate in a tightly sealed jar with a skim of oil on top for 1–2 weeks. You can also freeze pesto if you make it without the Parmesan cheese, which doesn't do well in the freezer. I like to freeze it in ice cube trays, which I unmold when frozen solid and store in a freezer bag.

HOW TO BLANCH VEGETABLES

To blanch vegetables, plunge them into rapidly boiling water and cook just until they're partially cooked and a brilliant color. Cooking time depends on the type of vegetable. In general, quick-cooking vegetables, such as asparagus, green beans, snow peas and broccoli florets, will take 1–2 minutes. Firmer vegetables, such as Brussels sprouts, will take 3–4 minutes, depending on the size. Plunge blanched vegetables immediately into ice-cold water to stop the cooking process and set the color. When thoroughly chilled, drain well.

SALAD NIÇOISE
for ONE

preparation time · 5 minutes
cooking time · 10 minutes (to boil egg)
makes · 1 serving

Canned tuna is a staple ingredient in many households. It's great in a sandwich (see Curried Tuna Salad–Stuffed Pita, page 36) and, as this Mediterranean-style recipe proves, also delicious in a salad. It calls for a boiled egg, which you can prepare ahead of time. I simply cook an extra egg alongside the one I'm having for breakfast one morning and cool, peel and store it in the refrigerator until needed.

ERIC'S OPTIONS
Substitute another type of seafood, such as salad shrimp or smoked salmon, for the tuna. Make the salad Greek-style by crumbling a little feta cheese on top.

1½ cups	organic mixed salad greens or chopped lettuce	375 mL
1	4 oz (120 g) can chunk tuna, drained well and coarsely flaked	1
1	hard-boiled egg, quartered	1
4–5	green beans, blanched and sliced in 2-inch (5 cm) pieces (see How to Blanch Vegetables, page 32)	4–5
4	cherry tomatoes, halved	4
6	black olives	6
1–2 Tbsp	homemade (see Herb and Garlic Vinaigrette, page 59) or store-bought vinaigrette salad dressing	15–30 mL

Place the salad greens in a shallow container. Top with the tuna, egg, beans, cherry tomatoes and olives. Pack the salad dressing in a separate small container and refrigerate both until lunchtime. Drizzle the salad with the dressing just before serving.

Salad Niçoise for One

WHAT'S VINAIGRETTE?

Traditionally, vinaigrette is a tangy mix of oil and vinegar in a ratio of 3 parts oil to 1 part vinegar. Depending on the tartness of the vinegar, this ratio can vary. For example, when using slightly sweet balsamic vinegar, less oil will be needed. Very acidic, everyday white vinegar may require more oil to balance its sharpness.

Lemon juice or other acidic liquids sometimes replace the vinegar. Herbs, garlic and spices are often added to enhance flavor, and Dijon mustard may be whisked in to help emulsify the oil and vinegar. With so many types of oil and vinegar available, you could make a different vinaigrette each day for weeks.

CURRIED TUNA
SALAD–STUFFED PITA

preparation time · 10 minutes
cooking time · none
makes · 2 servings

A curry-spiced twist on the classic sandwich.

ERIC'S OPTIONS
You can make the tuna salad the night before you need it. Refrigerate overnight and stuff the pita in the morning just before you go to work. Spice the tuna salad according to taste by using mild, medium or hot curry powder. Instead of pita bread, use 2 large crusty buns and make bunwiches.

1	6 oz (170 g) can chunk tuna (packed in water), drained well	1
1	celery rib, finely chopped	1
1	green onion, finely chopped	1
3 Tbsp	mayonnaise	45 mL
1 tsp	curry powder	5 mL
1 Tbsp	freshly squeezed lime juice	15 mL
to taste	salt and white pepper	to taste
2 cups	organic mixed salad greens	500 mL
1	pocketed pita, halved (see Note)	1

Place the tuna, celery, green onion, mayonnaise, curry powder, lime juice, salt and pepper in a bowl and mix well to combine. Divide the salad greens in half and stuff the pita pockets. Divide the tuna salad and stuff into the pitas. Wrap the stuffed pitas and chill until ready to serve.

NOTE
There are 2 main types of pita bread available: those that are puffed and have a pocket in the middle that's great for stuffing and those that are flat, with no pocket, which are often referred to as Greek-style pita bread.

SALMON SALAD WHOLE WHEAT BUNWICH with LEMON and DILL

preparation time · 5 minutes
cooking time · none
makes · 1 serving

The smaller cans of salmon available at most supermarkets these days are a perfect size to create a tasty sandwich for one. The fresh dill and lemon raise this a notch above the usual salmon salad.

ERIC'S OPTIONS
The salmon salad could be made the night before. Cover and keep refrigerated until ready to make your bunwich. If you don't care for dill, try another fresh or dried herb, such as tarragon or chives.

1	3½ oz (106 g) can salmon, drained well	1
1 Tbsp	mayonnaise	15 mL
1 tsp	freshly squeezed lemon juice	5 mL
1 tsp	chopped fresh dill, or pinch of dried dill	5 mL
to taste	freshly ground black pepper	to taste
1	whole wheat kaiser or burger bun, cut in half	1
2 tsp	butter, at room temperature	10 mL
1	lettuce leaf	1

Combine the salmon, mayonnaise, lemon juice, dill and pepper in a small bowl and mix well. Split and butter the bun, fill with the salmon salad, add the lettuce and replace the top of the bun. Wrap and refrigerate until lunchtime.

FIVE-MINUTE
FRIED RICE

preparation time · 10 minutes
cooking time · 5 minutes
makes · 2 servings

There's almost always leftover cooked rice in my refrigerator. I'm happy to see it, because it's great for making fried rice—a fine meal that's perfect for a workday lunch.

ERIC'S OPTIONS
For spicy fried rice, mix in hot Asian-style chili sauce to taste when adding the soy sauce.

1 Tbsp	vegetable oil	15 mL
1 cup	finely chopped vegetables, such as onion, celery, bell pepper, cabbage and carrot	250 mL
½ tsp	chopped garlic	2 mL
1½ cups	cooked rice	375 mL
½ cup	cooked shrimp or chopped cooked chicken, pork or beef	125 mL
¼ cup	frozen peas	60 mL
1–2 Tbsp	soy sauce, or to taste	15–30 mL
3 Tbsp	water or chicken stock	45 mL
to taste	freshly ground black pepper	to taste

Heat the oil in a nonstick skillet over medium-high heat. Add the chopped vegetables and stir-fry for 2 minutes. Add the remaining ingredients and stir-fry for 3 minutes, or until heated through and well combined. Cool the rice to room temperature, cover and store in the refrigerator. Reheat the next morning and pack in an insulated container or reheat the rice at lunchtime.

SMOKED TURKEY WRAP
with DRIED CRANBERRIES and PECANS

preparation time · 5 minutes
cooking time · none
makes · 1 serving

Smoked turkey is available at most supermarkets. It's deliciously complemented here by the earthy greens, tangy cranberries and rich-tasting pecans.

ERIC'S OPTIONS
Instead of smoked turkey, try another thinly sliced deli meat, such as regular turkey or ham. Instead of pecans, substitute walnuts or toasted, slivered almonds.

1	10-inch (25 cm) tortilla, white, whole wheat or flavored (see Note)	1
1–2 Tbsp	mayonnaise	15–30 mL
2–3 oz	thinly sliced smoked turkey	50–75 g
1 cup	organic mixed salad greens	250 mL
¼ cup	thinly sliced English cucumber	60 mL
2 Tbsp	dried cranberries	30 mL
1–2 Tbsp	pecan pieces	15–30 mL
to taste	freshly ground black pepper	to taste

Place the tortilla on your work surface and spread 1 side with the mayonnaise. Arrange the turkey, salad greens and cucumber in a row across the center of the tortilla. Sprinkle with the cranberries, pecans and black pepper. Fold the sides of the tortilla partially over the filling and then roll up. Wrap tightly in plastic wrap and store in the refrigerator. This wrap can be made the night the before you need it.

NOTE
To make tortillas easier to roll, heat for few seconds in the microwave before filling.

HOW TO STORE NUTS

Nuts, such as walnuts, pecans, almonds and cashews, have a high fat content, making them susceptible to going rancid if improperly stored. To prevent this, pack them in an airtight container and store in the refrigerator or freezer. Store shelled nuts in the refrigerator or freezer for 4–6 months, and nuts in the shell for 6–8 months. Storage times will be much shorter, of course, if the nuts you've bought weren't very fresh to begin with. Buy what you can use in a reasonable length of time from a retailer that sells a high volume of nuts and is constantly restocking with a fresh supply.

HOMEMADE GRANOLA BARS

preparation time	·	20 minutes
cooking time	·	25–30 minutes
makes	·	20 bars

These chewy bars are packed with energy-rich dried fruit and provide a tasty way to round off a workday or school lunch or to enjoy as an afternoon snack. The best part is that you control the ingredients that go into them, something you can't do with commercially made granola bars that are often filled with multiple types of sugar and preservatives.

ERIC'S OPTIONS
Substitute other dried fruits, such as chopped apricots, currants, dates or cherries, for some of the fruit called for in this recipe. Make a sweeter treat by substituting ½ cup (125 mL) chocolate chips for the same amount of dried fruit.

4 cups	quick-cooking oats	1 L
½ cup	golden brown sugar, packed	125 mL
½ cup	dried cranberries	125 mL
½ cup	raisins	125 mL
½ cup	currants	125 mL
¼ cup	unsweetened medium coconut flakes	60 mL
1 tsp	vanilla	5 mL
1 tsp	ground cinnamon	5 mL
½ tsp	salt	2 mL
½ cup	butter, melted	125 mL
1 cup	liquid honey, warmed	250 mL

Preheat the oven to 350°F (180°C). Cut a 13- x 13-inch (33 x 33 cm) piece of parchment paper and fit it into the bottom and up 2 sides of a 9- x 13-inch (23 x 33 cm) baking pan. (The parchment extending up the sides of the pan will help lift the granola out of the pan after baking.) Place the oats, brown sugar, cranberries, raisins, currants, coconut, vanilla, cinnamon and salt in a large bowl and stir to combine. Pour the melted butter and honey over the dry mixture and stir well to combine.

Instructions continued on the following page …

Press the mixture evenly into the prepared baking pan, packing it very, very tightly. Bake for 25–30 minutes, or until lightly golden on top and slightly firm to the touch. Cool to room temperature on a rack.

Loosen the granola from the sides of the pan with a paring knife. Using the edges of the parchment paper, lift the granola out of the pan and set on a cutting board. With a sharp, serrated knife, cut the granola into 20 bars. Store in a tightly sealed container at room temperature for 2–3 days, or freeze for up to a month. In either case, layer the bars between parchment or waxed paper if you need to stack them.

STORING DRIED FRUIT

Dried fruits, such as raisins, cranberries and currants, can be stored for 6 months or even more if properly handled and kept cool. Exposure to air and heat can cause dried fruit to become too dry, stale and hard. Once you've opened the package, transfer the unused portion of dried fruit to an airtight container and store in the refrigerator or cold storage area.

MAIN COURSE SOUPS AND SALADS

QUICK TOMATO SOUP
with PESTO and FETA

preparation time · 15 minutes
cooking time · 20 minutes
makes · 4 servings

Rich and herbaceous pesto, creamy feta and tangy tomato combine in this Mediterranean-style soup. Complete this meal in a bowl by serving it with thick slices of focaccia, Italian or olive bread.

ERIC'S OPTIONS
Instead of feta, top the soup with another cheese, such as crumbled goat cheese or grated Asiago. This soup, without the pesto and cheese, freezes well. Thaw in the refrigerator overnight, reheat, stir in the pesto, ladle into bowls and top with the cheese.

2 Tbsp	olive oil	30 mL
1	medium onion, halved and thinly sliced	1
1	garlic clove, crushed	1
2 Tbsp	tomato paste	30 mL
2 Tbsp	all-purpose flour	30 mL
2 cups	chicken or vegetable stock	500 mL
1	28 oz (796 mL) can diced tomatoes	1
½ tsp	sugar	2 mL
3 Tbsp	homemade or store-bought pesto (see About Pesto, page 31)	45 mL
to taste	salt and freshly ground black pepper	to taste
1 cup	crumbled feta cheese	250 mL

Pour the oil into a medium-sized pot and set over medium heat. Add the onion and garlic and cook until tender, about 5 minutes. Stir in the tomato paste and flour and cook for 1–2 minutes more. While stirring, slowly pour in the stock. Mix in the diced tomatoes and sugar. Bring the soup to a simmer and cook at a simmer for 10 minutes.

Purée the mixture in a food processor or with a hand-held immersion blender. Return the soup to a simmer and mix in the pesto; season with salt and pepper. Ladle the soup into heated bowls, sprinkle with the feta cheese and serve.

ABOUT FETA CHEESE

Traditionally made with sheep or goat milk, or a mix of both, feta is now also made with cow's milk. The cheese is prepared by curdling milk with rennet, an enzyme that coagulates the milk and creates curds that separate from the whey. The curds are drained, placed in perforated molds and pressed to create a solid cheese. It's then covered in brine and cured for several weeks, giving it a tangy flavor. When ready, the cheese will feel firm to somewhat firm depending on the fat content of the milk and the length of brining. It will also have the tender, crumbly texture that feta cheese is famous for.

MANHATTAN-STYLE CLAM CHOWDER

preparation time · 20 minutes
cooking time · 20 minutes
makes · 4 servings

Serve this sustaining, tomato-based chowder for supper on a cool, damp day.

ERIC'S OPTIONS
Use 2–3 medium, ripe fresh tomatoes, finely chopped, instead of canned diced tomatoes. Add the fresh tomatoes to the soup after pouring in the stock. If you have fresh tarragon, use 1 Tbsp (15 mL), chopped, in place of the dried tarragon.

2 Tbsp	butter	30 mL
1	medium onion, chopped	1
1	celery rib, chopped	1
1	small carrot, finely chopped	1
2½ cups	low-sodium chicken stock	625 mL
1	10 oz (284 mL) can clam nectar	1
1	10 oz (284 mL) can baby clams	1
1	14 oz (398 mL) can diced tomatoes	1
2	medium white-skinned potatoes, cubed	2
1 Tbsp	tomato paste	15 mL
to taste	salt and freshly ground black pepper	to taste
½ tsp	dried tarragon	2 mL
1	bay leaf	1

Melt the butter in a soup pot over medium heat. Add the onion, celery and carrot and cook until softened, about 5 minutes. Add the remaining ingredients and bring to a simmer. Simmer for 10–15 minutes, or until the potatoes are tender. Adjust the seasoning and serve.

AVGOLEMONO SOUP

preparation time · 15 minutes
cooking time · about 20 minutes
makes · 2 servings

This tangy Greek-style soup is flavored with lemon and thickened with a nutrient-filled egg. The rice and chicken make it a satisfying and filling meal. For supper, serve it with wedges of pita bread and a green salad.

ERIC'S OPTIONS

If you have leftover roasted chicken breast, cube it and use it instead of the raw chicken breast. You can also substitute an equal amount of raw boneless, skinless turkey breast. For added color, flavor and texture, mix ¼ cup (60 mL) of finely chopped fresh red bell pepper into the soup just before adding the egg mixture.

2½ cups	chicken stock	625 mL
¼ cup	long-grain white rice	60 mL
1	6 oz (175 g) boneless, skinless chicken breast, cut into small cubes	1
1	large egg	1
2 Tbsp	freshly squeezed lemon juice	30 mL
to taste	salt and white pepper	to taste
1	green onion, chopped	1

Place the stock, rice and chicken in a pot and bring to a boil. Lower the heat to a gentle simmer and cook until the rice is tender, about 10 minutes. Whisk the egg and lemon juice in a small bowl. Slowly drizzle ½ cup (125 mL) of the hot soup into the egg mixture, whisking constantly. Pour the warmed egg mixture into the soup in a thin stream, whisking continually. Cook until the soup just starts to thicken, about 1 minute. Season with salt and pepper. Ladle into warm bowls, sprinkle with green onion and serve.

BLACK BEAN and CORN SOUP with JACK CHEESE

preparation time · 15 minutes
cooking time · 6–7 minutes
makes · 2 servings

This is a mildly spicy, stick-to-your-ribs kind of soup. I like to serve it with warm tortillas, which I tear into chunks and dunk into the soup.

ERIC'S OPTIONS
For added color, flavor and texture, mix ¼ cup (60 mL) of finely chopped fresh red bell pepper into the soup when adding the corn. For a spicy/smoky taste, replace the hot pepper sauce with half a chipotle pepper, puréeing it with the beans. (Chipotle peppers are smoked jalapeño peppers that are sold in cans in the Mexican food aisle of most supermarkets. Store any unused peppers in a tightly sealed jar in the refrigerator; they'll keep for several weeks.)

1	14 oz (398 mL) can black beans, drained and rinsed	1
1½ cups	chicken or vegetable stock	375 mL
1 Tbsp	all-purpose flour	15 mL
½ cup	frozen corn kernels	125 mL
¼ tsp	chili powder	1 mL
¼ tsp	ground cumin	1 mL
to taste	hot pepper sauce, such as Tabasco	to taste
to taste	salt	to taste
⅓ cup	grated Monterey Jack cheese	75 mL
1	green onion, chopped	1

Pulse the black beans, stock and flour in a food processor or blender until the beans are puréed. Transfer the mixture to a small soup pot and set over medium heat. Add the corn, chili powder, cumin and hot pepper sauce and bring to a simmer; simmer for 5 minutes. Season with salt and ladle into warm soup bowls. Sprinkle with the cheese and green onion and serve immediately.

RED ONION SOUP
with BRIE

preparation time	20 minutes
cooking time	about 30 minutes
makes	4 servings

Serve this luscious soup with the remainder of the red wine you use to make it, and any stress remaining from your workday will soon fade away.

ERIC'S OPTIONS
You can substitute yellow onions for the red onions.
For a more intense-tasting cheese, instead of brie, top the soup with slices of a blue-veined cheese, such as cambozola.

2 Tbsp	butter	30 mL
3	medium red onions, cut in half and thinly sliced	3
1	garlic clove, chopped	1
1 Tbsp	all-purpose flour	15 mL
1 Tbsp	Dijon mustard	15 mL
½ cup	red wine	125 mL
4½ cups	beef stock	1.125 L
½ tsp	dried thyme	2 mL
to taste	salt and freshly ground black pepper	to taste
4	1-inch-thick (2.5 cm) slices French bread, toasted	4
8–12	slices brie cheese	8–12

Melt the butter in a pot over medium heat. Add the onions and cook, stirring occasionally, for 10 minutes, or until the onions are caramel-like and sticky. Stir in the garlic and cook for a few seconds more. Mix in the flour and mustard; slowly add the wine, whisking constantly. Stir in the stock and thyme and bring the soup to a gentle simmer. Continue to simmer for 15 minutes; season with salt and pepper.

Preheat the broiler, setting the oven rack 6 inches (15 cm) underneath it. Place 4 heatproof soup bowls on a baking sheet. Put a toasted slice of French bread in the bottom of each bowl. Ladle in the soup. Top each bowl with 2–3 slices of cheese. Place under the broiler and broil until the cheese is melted. Serve immediately.

CHICKPEA and SPINACH SOUP

preparation time · 15 minutes
cooking time · 16–17 minutes
makes · 4 servings

This hearty soup is quick to make because there's minimal chopping. If you use vegetable stock and skip the cheese, this soup is vegan.

ERIC'S OPTIONS
Substitute a similar-sized can of white kidney beans for the chickpeas. Instead of spinach, chop and mix 2 cups (500 mL) of Swiss chard into the soup.

2 Tbsp	olive oil	30 mL
1	medium onion, diced	1
½	large red bell pepper, diced	½
1–2	garlic cloves, crushed	1–2
1 tsp	dried oregano	5 mL
2 Tbsp	tomato paste	30 mL
4 cups	chicken or vegetable stock	1 L
1	19 oz (540 mL) can chickpeas, rinsed and drained well	1
2 cups	fresh spinach leaves, thickly sliced	500 mL
to taste	salt and freshly ground black pepper	to taste
to taste	freshly grated Parmesan cheese	to taste

Heat the oil in a soup pot over medium heat. Add the onion, bell pepper and garlic and cook for 3–4 minutes. Mix in the oregano and tomato paste and cook 2 minutes longer. Add the stock and chickpeas, bring to a simmer and simmer for 10 minutes. Add the spinach and cook until it just starts to wilt, about 1 minute. Season with salt and pepper. Ladle the soup into bowls, sprinkle with Parmesan cheese and serve.

ORGANIC SALAD GREENS with CANDIED SALMON, GOAT CHEESE and BLUEBERRIES

preparation time	·	10 minutes
cooking time	·	none
makes	·	4 servings

This elegant salad is wonderful on a warm summer day—when turning on the stove is the last thing anyone wants to do. Candied salmon is available at some supermarkets and specialty seafood stores. To make it, salmon is brined and then hot-smoked, fully cooking the fish. During the process it's soaked or basted with a sweetener, such as brown sugar, honey or maple syrup, giving it a candy-like look and taste.

ERIC'S OPTIONS
If you can't find candied salmon, use slices of cold-smoked salmon (most often called lox), or coarsely flaked hot-smoked salmon or trout. Use baby spinach or chopped romaine or leaf lettuce in the salad instead of organic mixed salad greens. For a fruitier taste, make the salad dressing with raspberry vinegar instead of balsamic.

2 Tbsp	balsamic vinegar	30 mL
3 Tbsp	extra virgin olive oil	45 mL
1 tsp	Dijon mustard	5 mL
1 tsp	honey	5 mL
to taste	salt and freshly ground black pepper	to taste
6–8 cups	organic mixed salad greens	1.5–2 L
½ lb	candied salmon, coarsely flaked	250 g
5 oz	soft goat cheese, crumbled	150 g
1 cup	fresh blueberries	250 mL

Place the vinegar, oil, mustard, honey, salt and pepper in a large bowl and whisk to combine. Add the salad greens and gently toss to coat. Divide the greens among 4 plates. Arrange the salmon, goat cheese and blueberries on top of the greens and serve.

SPINACH SALAD with SMOKED TURKEY and CANTALOUPE

preparation time · 15 minutes
cooking time · none
makes · 4 servings

Deep-green, earthy spinach, sweet cantaloupe and smoke-infused turkey are a delicious combination in this salad flavored with a honey garlic dressing. Smoked turkey is available at most supermarkets, usually in the deli section.

ERIC'S OPTIONS
Use organic mixed salad greens or chopped romaine or leaf lettuce instead of baby spinach. For a tropical taste, replace the melon with a ripe medium papaya, peeled, seeded and cubed. Substitute smoked chicken or ham for the turkey.

3 Tbsp	olive oil	45 mL
2 Tbsp	freshly squeezed lemon juice	30 mL
1 Tbsp	honey	15 mL
1	large garlic clove, crushed	1
1 tsp	Dijon mustard	5 mL
to taste	salt and fresh ground black pepper	to taste
6–8 cups	baby spinach	1.5 – 2 L
½	medium cantaloupe, peeled and cubed	½
1 cup	cubed smoked turkey	250 mL
⅓ cup	pecan halves	75 mL

Place the olive oil, lemon juice, honey, garlic, mustard, salt and pepper in a large bowl and whisk to combine. Add the spinach and toss to coat. Divide the spinach among 4 dinner plates. Artfully top with the cantaloupe, turkey and pecans and serve.

ABOUT CANTALOUPE

"True" cantaloupe has a rough, non-netted skin and aromatic flesh. It's widely grown in Europe, but not in North America. You can find "true" cantaloupe for sale at some farmers' markets and fine food stores.

Most cantaloupes sold in North American supermarkets are actually muskmelons, which have a netted rind. When ripe, the rind will turn from green to a slightly golden/tan color and the orange flesh will be very juicy.

When buying cantaloupe, true or not, choose sweetly aromatic ones that feel heavy for their size. Avoid those that have a musty odor or bruising. Cantaloupe, unlike some fruit such as bananas, doesn't continue to ripen after it's been picked. However, you can improve the taste of slightly under-ripe cantaloupe by leaving it out at room temperature for a few days. This will soften the flesh, making it juicer. Store ripe or cut and wrapped cantaloupe in the refrigerator; if it's in very good condition it will keep for several days. Cantaloupe is a good source of vitamins A and C and potassium.

WHOLE WHEAT PASTA SALAD
with TUNA and VEGETABLES

preparation time · 15 minutes
cooking time · 8–10 minutes
makes · 4 servings

This healthy salad is rich in fiber, protein and vitamin C—and it's delicious!

ERIC'S OPTIONS
Instead of penne, use any other bite-sized whole wheat pasta, such as rotini or bow-tie. If you prefer regular pasta, use it instead of whole wheat. Instead of snow peas, use 24 snap peas or small broccoli florets, blanched.

½ lb	whole wheat penne	250 g
¼ cup	store-bought or homemade pesto (see About Pesto, page 31)	60 mL
3 Tbsp	red wine vinegar	45 mL
1 Tbsp	extra virgin olive oil	15 mL
½ tsp	sugar	2 mL
to taste	salt and freshly ground black pepper	to taste
1	6 oz (170 g) can chunk tuna, drained and flaked	1
12	cherry tomatoes, halved	12
24–30	snow peas, blanched (see How to Blanch Vegetables, page 32)	24–30
1	medium carrot, peeled and grated	1

Bring a large of pot of lightly salted water to a boil. Add the pasta and cook until just tender, about 8–10 minutes. Drain the pasta well, cool in ice-cold water and then drain well again. Place the pasta in a bowl, add the remaining ingredients and gently toss to combine. Cover and refrigerate. Toss again just before serving.

SHRIMP CAESAR SALAD WRAPS

preparation time · 10 minutes
cooking time · none
makes · 4 servings

Here's a no-fuss Caesar salad you can eat in the hand, with the added luxury of shrimp.

ERIC'S OPTIONS
If you have hearty eaters, double the recipe and serve 2 wraps per person. Use baby spinach to make the salad instead of chopped romaine. Use 2 grilled and chilled chicken breasts, thinly sliced, instead of the shrimp.

⅓ cup	store-bought or homemade Caesar salad dressing (see page 58)	75 ml
6–8 cups	chopped romaine lettuce	1.5–2 L
⅓ lb	cooked salad shrimp (see About Salad Shrimp, page 27)	170 g
¼ cup	freshly grated Parmesan cheese	60 mL
4	10-inch (25 cm) tortilla shells	4

Place the salad dressing in a large bowl; add the romaine, shrimp and cheese and toss to combine. Arrange the salad down the center of each tortilla. Fold the sides of the tortilla partially over the salad and then roll up. Cut each wrap in half at a slight angle and arrange on plates. Serve additional dressing alongside for dipping, if desired.

CAESAR SALAD DRESSING

preparation time · 5 minutes
cooking time · none
makes · 1¾ cups (425 mL)

Why buy Caesar salad dressing at the supermarket when you can whirl together a superior-tasting version at home in just a few minutes? This dressing also makes a tasty dip for a tray of crisp, raw vegetables.

ERIC'S OPTIONS
Use 4 tsp (20 mL) anchovy paste instead of whole anchovies.

1¼ cups	mayonnaise	310 mL
2	anchovy fillets	2
3	garlic cloves, thickly sliced	3
2 Tbsp	extra virgin olive oil	30 mL
1 Tbsp	Dijon mustard	15 mL
1 Tbsp	red wine vinegar	15 mL
1 Tbsp	freshly squeezed lemon juice	15 mL
2 tsp	Worcestershire sauce	10 mL
½ tsp	hot pepper sauce, such as Tabasco	2 mL
1 tsp	coarsely ground black pepper, or to taste	5 mL
2 Tbsp	cold water	30 mL

Place all the ingredients in a food processor or blender. Pulse until well combined. Transfer to a tightly sealed jar and store in the refrigerator for up to 2 weeks.

HERB and
GARLIC VINAIGRETTE

preparation time	·	10 minutes
cooking time	·	none
makes	·	1 cup (250 mL)

I keep this tasty and aromatic vinaigrette on hand in the refrigerator to drizzle on salads.

ERIC'S OPTIONS
If you find this vinaigrette too tart, shake in a pinch of sugar or drizzle of honey when making it.

¾ cup	extra virgin olive oil	175 mL
¼ cup	white or red wine vinegar	60 mL
1–2	garlic cloves, minced	1–2
1 tsp	Dijon mustard	5 mL
½ tsp	granulated sugar	2 mL
½ tsp	dried oregano	2 mL
½ tsp	dried basil	2 mL
¼ tsp	paprika	1 mL
pinch	crushed chili flakes	pinch
to taste	salt and freshly ground black pepper	to taste

Place all the ingredients in a jar with a tight-fitting lid. Shake vigorously until well combined. Store in the refrigerator for up to 1 week. Shake well before using.

ROMAINE HEARTS with SHRIMP and GRAPEFRUIT

preparation time · 10 minutes
cooking time · none
makes · 4 servings

Here's a light and refreshing main course salad. Romaine hearts are, as their name suggests, the well-trimmed, center portion of the lettuce. They're sold in bags at most supermarkets.

ERIC'S OPTIONS
Instead of shrimp, top the salad with flaked pieces of hot-smoked salmon.

¼ cup	freshly squeezed grapefruit juice	60 mL
3 Tbsp	extra virgin olive oil	45 mL
2 tsp	liquid honey	10 mL
to taste	salt and freshly ground black pepper	to taste
2	romaine hearts, chopped	2
24–32	peeled, cooked medium shrimp (see Note)	24–32
2	medium grapefruit, peel and pith removed, halved and thinly sliced	2

Place the grapefruit juice, oil, honey, salt and pepper in a salad bowl. Add the romaine and toss to coat the lettuce. Divide the romaine among 4 plates. Arrange the shrimp and grapefruit slices on top and serve.

NOTE
Peeled, cooked shrimp are available at most supermarkets.

NIFTY NOODLES

CHAPTER FOUR

THAI-STYLE NOODLES
with COCONUT, CURRY and SHRIMP

preparation time	·	5 minutes
cooking time	·	10–12 minutes
makes	·	4 servings

I consider this dish mildly spicy. If you like things hotter, when making the sauce for the noodles incrementally increase the amount of curry paste in small amounts until you achieve the desired level of spiciness. Green curry paste, coconut milk, fish sauce and rice noodles—the wider style is preferable for this dish—are available in the Asian food aisle of most supermarkets.

ERIC'S OPTIONS
Two thinly sliced, cooked chicken breasts could replace the shrimp in this recipe. If desired, you could also add a cup (250 mL) or so of thinly sliced vegetables, such as carrots, snow peas and/or bell peppers. Add the vegetables just before you simmer the coconut sauce for 5 minutes.

1	14 oz (398 mL) can coconut milk	1
2 tsp	green Thai curry paste	10 mL
2 Tbsp	fish sauce	30 mL
1 tsp	brown sugar	5 mL
2–3 Tbsp	freshly squeezed lime juice	30–45 mL
½ lb	rice noodles	250 g
½ lb	cooked salad shrimp	250 g
¼ cup	chopped fresh cilantro or green onion	60 mL
for garnish	lime wedges	for garnish

Bring a large pot of water to a boil. Meanwhile, place the coconut milk, curry paste, fish sauce, brown sugar and lime juice in a wok or large skillet and set over medium-high heat. Bring to a boil, then lower the heat until the mixture gently simmers. Cook at a simmer for 5 minutes.

When the sauce has simmered for 5 minutes, add the noodles to the boiling water and cook for 1 minute, or until just tender. Drain the noodles well and add them, along with the shrimp, to the sauce. Gently toss and cook for 2 minutes more. Divide the noodles among 4 plates or bowls. Sprinkle with the chopped cilantro or green onion and serve, garnished with lime wedges.

ABOUT CURRY PASTE

Curry paste is a flavorful ingredient that's widely used in a range of Asian-style dishes. Like curry powder, it's made with a mix of spices, but it's in the form of a paste made with oil or other liquids and fresh ingredients, such as hot chilies and garlic. Curry paste is sold in jars and pouches at Asian markets and most supermarkets. It may simply be labeled "curry paste," available in mild, medium and hot, and there are also regional variations. Madras curry paste features ingredients such as red chilies, coriander and cumin, and there are Thai-style green, red and yellow curry pastes, which get their name from the color of the chilies and other ingredients used to make them.

SEAFOOD NOODLE BOWL

preparation time · 20 minutes
cooking time · about 12 minutes
makes · 4 servings

Assorted seafood in a broth redolent with ginger—this is a dish for seafood lovers!

ERIC'S OPTIONS

Instead of salmon, try another cubed fish, such as halibut or snapper. If you don't like spicy foods, reduce or omit the chili sauce. Rice noodles can be substituted for the egg noodles.

3½ cups	chicken or vegetable stock	875 mL
1	garlic clove, chopped	1
1 Tbsp	chopped fresh ginger	15 mL
2 Tbsp	soy sauce	30 mL
1 tsp	hot Asian-style chili sauce	5 mL
1	small carrot, halved lengthwise and cut into thin slices	1
12–16	small scallops	12–16
½ lb	salmon fillet, cubed	250 g
¼ lb	cooked salad shrimp	125 g
2	baby bok choy, separated into leaves and coarsely chopped	2
½ lb	Chinese-style egg noodles	250 g

Bring a large pot of water to a boil. Meanwhile, place the stock, garlic, ginger, soy sauce, chili sauce and carrot in a medium pot and bring to a gentle simmer. Simmer for 5 minutes. Add the scallops and salmon and simmer until cooked through, about 3 minutes. Add the shrimp and bok choy and cook until the shrimp are heated through and the bok choy is just wilted, about 2 minutes.

While the seafood is cooking, add the noodles to the boiling water and cook until just tender, about 1 minute. Drain the noodles well and divide them among 4 large soup bowls. Spoon the seafood/vegetable mixture and broth over the noodles, dividing the seafood equally among the bowls, and serve.

ASIAN-STYLE VEGETABLE NOODLE BOWL

preparation time	·	20 minutes
cooking time	·	about 10 minutes
makes	·	4 servings

A vegetarian noodle bowl filled with colorful vegetables swimming in a tasty broth.

ERIC'S OPTIONS
Make this a meaty soup by topping it with heated slices of the barbecued pork or duck you can find in Asian markets. If you prefer rice noodles, use them instead of egg noodles.

3½ cups	vegetable stock	875 mL
1	garlic clove, chopped	1
1 Tbsp	chopped fresh ginger	15 mL
2 Tbsp	soy sauce	30 mL
1 tsp	hot Asian-style chili sauce	5 mL
1	medium carrot, halved lengthwise and thinly sliced	1
1	medium red bell pepper, halved and thinly sliced	1
1	14 oz (398 mL) can cut young corn (see Note, page 67)	1
3	baby bok choy, separated into leaves and coarsely chopped	3
½ lb	Chinese-style egg noodles	250 g
⅓ cup	chopped fresh cilantro or green onion	75 mL
1 cup	bean sprouts	250 mL

Instructions follow on page 67 ...

ASIAN-STYLE VEGETABLE NOODLE BOWL (CONTINUED)

Bring a large pot of water to a boil. Meanwhile, place the stock, garlic, ginger, soy sauce, chili sauce and carrot in a medium pot and bring to a gentle simmer. Simmer for 5 minutes. Add the bell pepper, corn and bok choy and cook 2–3 minutes longer.

While the vegetables are cooking, add the noodles to the boiling water and cook until just tender, about 1 minute. Drain the noodles well and divide them among 4 large soup bowls. Ladle the broth and vegetables over the noodles, top with the cilantro or green onions and bean sprouts and serve steaming hot.

NOTE
Canned young (also called baby) corn is sold in the Asian food aisle of most supermarkets. It is sold in whole small cobs or cut into pieces, the latter being a convenient, no-slicing-required ingredient to add to a range of dishes.

MEATBALLS in SOUR CREAM GRAVY with PARSLEY NOODLES

preparation time · 10 minutes
cooking time · about 20 minutes
makes · 4 servings

This is a delectable combination of buttery noodles and meatballs smothered in a rich, tangy, sour cream gravy.

ERIC'S OPTIONS
Instead of egg noodles, serve the meatballs on a bed of Garlic Mashed Yukon Gold Potatoes (page 176).

2½ cups	beef stock	625 mL
¼ cup	all-purpose flour	60 mL
½ cup	sour cream	125 mL
to taste	salt and freshly ground black pepper	to taste
24–32	frozen store-bought or homemade meatballs (see Large Batch Roast and Freeze Meatballs, page 159), thawed	24–32
1	11 oz (350 g) package egg noodles (see Note)	1
2 Tbsp	melted butter	30 mL
2 Tbsp	chopped fresh parsley	30 mL

Bring a large pot of lightly salted water to a boil. Meanwhile, place the stock and flour in a medium pot and whisk until there are no lumps. Bring to a boil over medium-high heat, then reduce the heat to a gentle simmer. Whisk in the sour cream, salt and pepper. Add the meatballs to the sauce, return to a simmer and cook for 10 minutes.

While the meatballs simmer, add the noodles to the boiling water and cook until tender, about 5 minutes. Drain the noodles well and toss them with the butter and parsley. Divide them among 4 plates or shallow bowls, spoon the meatballs and gravy overtop and serve immediately.

NOTE
The egg noodles used in this recipe are the broad European-style egg noodles, not the thin Chinese-style ones. You'll find them in most supermarkets in the pasta aisle.

SHAPING GROUND MEAT

Thoroughly wash your hands before and after handling any ground meat. When shaping the meat, be careful not to overmix it. The meat will compact and become quite firm when cooked—not the tender texture you want to have in a good meatball or burger.

Moisten your hands with cold water before shaping the meat—it will provide a barrier and prevent the meat from sticking to your hands. When you're done, use hot soapy water to clean all surfaces that come in contact with the raw meat.

WHOLE WHEAT ROTINI PRIMAVERA

preparation time · 20 minutes
cooking time · 15 minutes
makes · 4 servings

Primavera is an Italian term that means "springtime style." In culinary terms, it refers to any dish served with fresh vegetables—an apt description of this colorful pasta.

ERIC'S OPTIONS
Instead of rotini, use another bite-sized pasta, such as rigatoni or penne, or use regular pasta instead of whole wheat. If you like mushrooms, slice and add 6–8 medium white or brown ones when sautéing the vegetables.

1 lb	whole wheat rotini	500 g
2 Tbsp	olive oil	30 mL
1	medium onion, halved and sliced	1
1	small yellow or orange bell pepper, halved and thinly sliced	1
1	small zucchini, halved lengthwise and sliced	1
1½ cups	small broccoli florets	375 mL
1–2	garlic cloves, chopped	1–2
2 cups	store-bought or homemade tomato-based sauce (see Freezer Pasta Sauce, page 76)	500 mL
½ cup	chicken or vegetable stock	125 mL
¼ cup	chopped fresh basil	60 mL
⅓ cup	freshly grated Parmesan cheese	75 mL
to taste	salt and freshly ground black pepper	to taste

Cook the pasta in a large pot of lightly salted boiling water until just tender, about 8–10 minutes. Meanwhile, heat the oil in a large skillet over medium-high heat and add the onion, bell pepper, zucchini, broccoli and garlic. Cook, stirring, for 3–4 minutes. Add the pasta sauce and stock and bring to a simmer. Simmer until the vegetables are just tender, about 4–5 minutes.

When the pasta is cooked, drain it, reserving ½ cup (125 mL) of the cooking liquid. Add the pasta, reserved cooking liquid, basil, cheese, salt and pepper to the skillet. Toss to combine and serve immediately.

LINGUINI with MIXED PEAS and ARTICHOKES

preparation time · 20 minutes
cooking time · about 15 minutes
makes · 4 servings

Cherry tomatoes, fresh basil, artichoke hearts and a vibrant trio of peas give this pasta a springtime feel. Since all the ingredients are now available year round, you can make this dish and enjoy that feeling even in January.

ERIC'S OPTIONS

If desired, provide some extra virgin olive oil and a bowl of Parmesan cheese for drizzling and sprinkling on the pasta at the table. Instead of linguini, use another noodle, such as spaghetti or fettuccini. Instead of chopped fresh basil and garlic, add 2–3 Tbsp (30–45 mL) of store-bought or homemade pesto (see About Pesto, page 31).

¾ lb	linguini	375 g
3 Tbsp	extra virgin olive oil	45 mL
1–2	garlic cloves, chopped	1–2
1	14 oz (398 mL) can artichoke hearts, drained and quartered	1
16–20	snap peas, trimmed	16–20
16–20	snow peas, trimmed	16–20
1 cup	chicken or vegetable stock	250 mL
½ cup	frozen peas	125 mL
12	cherry tomatoes, halved	12
⅓ cup	freshly grated Parmesan cheese	75 mL
¼ cup	chopped fresh basil	60 mL
to taste	salt and freshly ground black pepper	to taste

Bring a large pot of lightly salted water to a boil. Add the linguini and cook until tender, about 8–10 minutes. Meanwhile, heat the olive oil in a large skillet over medium heat and add the garlic, artichokes, snap peas and snow peas. Cook, stirring, for 2–3 minutes. Add the stock and bring to a simmer.

Drain the pasta, reserving ½ cup (125 mL) of the cooking liquid. Add the pasta, reserved cooking liquid, frozen peas, cherry tomatoes, Parmesan, basil, salt and pepper to the skillet. Toss to combine, heat through for 1–2 minutes and serve.

SPAGHETTI
with QUICK MEAT SAUCE

preparation time · 5 minutes
cooking time · about 15 minutes
makes · 4 servings

This is a fast and easy supper that requires only a few ingredients. Serve it with garlic bread and a green or Caesar salad for a satisfying meal.

ERIC'S OPTIONS
This sauce is great with just about any type of pasta, such as linguini, rigatoni or ravioli. Instead of beef, use ground turkey.

1 lb	lean ground beef	500 g
3 cups	store-bought or homemade pasta sauce (see Freezer Pasta Sauce, page 76)	750 mL
½ cup	beef stock or water	125 mL
2–3 Tbsp	store-bought or homemade pesto (see About Pesto, page 31)	30–45 mL
1 lb	spaghetti	500 g
to taste	freshly grated Parmesan cheese	to taste

Brown the beef in a medium-sized pot over medium heat. Cook, stirring to break up the meat, until the beef is entirely cooked through and is no longer pink, about 5 minutes. Meanwhile, bring a large pot of lightly salted water to a boil. When the meat is cooked, drain off the excess fat. Add the pasta sauce, stock and pesto. Bring to a simmer and cook for 10 minutes.

While the sauce is simmering, cook the pasta in the boiling water until just tender, about 8–10 minutes. Drain well and divide among 4 pasta bowls. Spoon the sauce overtop. Serve with a bowl of freshly grated Parmesan cheese. Diners can top the pasta with as much, or as little, cheese as they like.

PASTA COOKING TIPS

When boiling pasta, some people add oil to the water to prevent the strands from sticking together. I don't recommend adding oil because it will coat the pasta and create a slippery surface that prevents sauce from clinging to it. And the truth is that you simply don't need oil if you use a generous amount of water to cook the pasta. When cooked in a small amount of water, starch from the pasta will concentrate and cause it to become sticky, glue together and cook unevenly. For every pound (500 g) of pasta, fresh or dried, I bring at least 1 gallon (4 L) of water to a boil. Pasta doesn't contain salt, so I also add 1 Tbsp (15 mL) of salt to the water. Italian cooks say that pasta should be cooked *al dente*, which means "to the bite." When you bite into it, it should have a slight resistance, but it shouldn't have a hard, uncooked center. The only way to gauge that is to taste the pasta as it cooks.

FREEZER
PASTA SAUCE

preparation time · 30 minutes
cooking time · 40 minutes
makes · about 16 cups

Make this tasty sauce on a day off and you'll be able to freeze individual packages for topping any type of cooked pasta, whether it's ravioli, linguini or rotini. Any ripe, red tomato is fine, but Roma (also called plum) tomatoes have thick flesh, small seeds and a rich flavor, which makes them especially good for sauce.

ERIC'S OPTIONS
If you prefer a chunky sauce, don't purée after simmering. Simmer 24–30 cooked, store-bought or homemade meatballs (see Large Batch Roast and Freeze Meatballs, page 159) in 4 cups (1 L) of this sauce for 10 minutes and you'll have a tasty spaghetti topping that serves 4.

12 lb	ripe, red tomatoes	5.5 kg
⅓ cup	olive oil	75 mL
4	medium onions, finely chopped	4
2	large celery ribs, finely chopped	2
4–6	garlic cloves, chopped	4–6
2 cups	chicken or vegetable stock or water	500 mL
2 tsp	granulated sugar	10 mL
¼ cup	tomato paste	60 mL
to taste	salt and freshly ground black pepper	to taste
3	bay leaves	3
1 Tbsp	dried oregano	15 mL
1 Tbsp	dried basil	15 mL
¼–½ tsp	crushed chili flakes (optional)	1–2 mL

Bring 5 inches (12 cm) of water to a boil in a large, wide pot. Cut the stem section out of each tomato and mark a shallow X at the blossom end. Immerse the tomatoes, a few at a time, in the boiling water for 1 minute, or until the skins just start to slip off. Transfer the tomatoes to a large tray with a slotted spoon and repeat with the remaining tomatoes. When the tomatoes are cool enough to handle, peel off and discard the skins.

Cut the tomatoes in half lengthwise. Set a sieve over a bowl. Squeeze the seeds out of the tomatoes into the sieve. Discard the seeds and reserve the liquid in the bowl. Coarsely chop the seeded tomatoes.

Place the oil in a large, heavy-bottomed pot over medium heat. Add the onion, celery and garlic and cook until tender, about 5 minutes. Add the chopped tomatoes, reserved liquid, stock, sugar, tomato paste, salt, pepper, bay leaves, oregano, basil and chili flakes, if using. Bring the mixture to a gentle simmer and cook for 30 minutes, or until it looks like a chunky tomato sauce. Remove and discard the bay leaves, and then purée the sauce in a food processor or with a hand-held immersion blender. Cool to room temperature. Divide among containers, seal tightly, label and freeze for up to 6 months. Thaw before using.

CHEESY TORTELLINI CASSEROLE

preparation time · 20 minutes
cooking time · about 10 minutes
makes · 6 servings

This hearty, cheese-rich casserole can be readied in advance and baked later—see Eric's Options, below, for instructions.

ERIC'S OPTIONS

Sprinkle the top of the casserole with a little chopped fresh basil or parsley just before serving. To make this casserole in advance and bake later, cool to room temperature after pouring on the sauce and sprinkling on the Parmesan cheese. Cover and store in the refrigerator for up to 1 day, or tightly wrap, label and freeze until needed. Thaw in the refrigerator overnight before baking, adding 5–10 minutes to the baking time to compensate for it being chilled. You can also make this in individual serving dishes and freeze; baking time will be about 25–30 minutes.

1	1½ lb (750 g) package cheese or meat-filled rainbow (three-color) tortellini	1
3 Tbsp	butter	45 mL
¼ cup	all-purpose flour	60 mL
3½ cups	warm milk	875 mL
¼ cup	chopped fresh basil or parsley	60 mL
1 cup	grated Asiago cheese	250 mL
1 cup	grated mozzarella cheese	250 mL
to taste	salt and white pepper	to taste
¼ cup	freshly grated Parmesan cheese	60 mL

Preheat the oven to 350°F (180°C). Bring a large pot of lightly salted water to a boil. Add the tortellini and cook until just tender, about 7–8 minutes depending on the brand. Meanwhile, melt the butter in a pot over medium heat. Stir in the flour until well combined. Slowly whisk in the milk. Cook, whisking constantly, until the mixture comes to a simmer and slightly thickens (take care it doesn't burn on the bottom). Remove the sauce from the heat and stir in the basil or parsley, Asiago and mozzarella; season with salt and pepper.

Drain the tortellini well and place in a 9- × 13-inch (3.5 L) casserole dish. Spoon the sauce overtop; sprinkle with the Parmesan cheese. Bake for 25–30 minutes, or until golden brown and bubbling.

ABOUT GRATED CHEESE

Before grating cheese, make sure it's well chilled; that makes it firmer and easier to grate. Expect ¼ lb (125 g) of cheese to yield about 1 cup (250 mL) of grated cheese. Grated cheese melts more evenly and quickly than cubes or chunks; add it to sauces at the end of cooking and use just enough heat to melt and mix it in. If heated too long, cheese can toughen and the fat may separate out and rise to the surface.

TORTELLINI ALFREDO

preparation time · 5 minutes
cooking time · about 10 minutes
makes · 4 generous servings

This rich, creamy comfort food is a treat that appeals to all ages.

ERIC'S OPTIONS
Use any filled pasta you like, such as ravioli or agnolotti, boiling it for the length of time suggested on the package. For fettuccini Alfredo, replace the tortellini with 1 lb (500 g) of fettuccini.

1	1 ½ lb (750 g) package cheese or meat-filled rainbow (three-color) tortellini	1
2 cups	whipping cream	500 mL
1–2	garlic cloves, crushed	1–2
1 tsp	dried oregano	5 mL
⅓ cup	freshly grated Parmesan cheese, plus some for the table	75 mL
to taste	salt and freshly ground black pepper	to taste

Bring a large pot of lightly salted water to a boil. Add the tortellini and cook until just tender, about 7–8 minutes depending on the brand. While the pasta cooks, place the cream, garlic and oregano in a very large skillet over medium heat. Bring to a simmer and mix in the cheese.

Drain the tortellini, reserving ½ cup (125 mL) of the cooking liquid. Add the tortellini, reserved cooking liquid, salt and pepper to the cream mixture and gently toss to combine. Serve immediately with additional Parmesan cheese for sprinkling on top.

SLOW COOKER SUPPERS

CHAPTER FIVE

HEARTY BARLEY
SOUP

preparation time · 25 minutes
cooking time · 8 hours
makes · 8 servings

Here's a tasty way to use up leftover cooked beef or lamb. It makes a fine meal served with thick slices of whole wheat bread. Chop the vegetables the night before so you can quickly get the soup on to cook the next morning. Freeze any leftover soup in individual servings that you can reheat for a meal later on.

ERIC'S OPTIONS
If you don't have leftover cooked meat to use in this recipe, use raw beef or lamb stewing meat, cut into small cubes. For a vegetarian soup, replace the cubed beef or lamb with 2 ripe medium tomatoes, chopped, and use vegetable stock instead of the beef stock.

¾ cup	diced turnip	175 mL
¾ cup	diced carrot	175 mL
¾ cup	diced celery	175 mL
¾ cup	diced onion	175 mL
1	garlic clove, chopped	1
½ cup	pot barley	125 mL
2 Tbsp	tomato paste	30 mL
2 cups	cubed cooked beef or lamb	500 mL
2	bay leaves	2
½ tsp	dried thyme	2 mL
8 cups	beef stock	2 L
to taste	salt and freshly ground black pepper	to taste
¼ cup	chopped parsley	60 mL

Combine everything except the parsley in your slow cooker. Cover and cook on the low setting for 8 hours. Just before serving, swirl in the parsley, taste the soup and add more salt and pepper if needed.

WHAT'S A SLOW COOKER?

This electrical appliance, which has been around since the 1970s, has had a resurgence in popularity over the last few years. This isn't surprising: with our ever-busier lives, this gadget can certainly make midweek meal preparation a lot easier. For the most part, you can simply put your ingredients in the slow cooker in the morning, let them cook all day while you're away and come home to a delicious home-cooked dinner.

Slow cookers consist of a metal container that holds a thick ceramic pot. A heating element in the walls of the metal container surrounds the ceramic pot, but doesn't touch it. When the element heats up, it evenly and slowly cooks the food and, because it's not touching the pot, there's no potential for the food to stick and burn. As the food warms, steam builds up, rises and falls back onto the food, keeping it moist and preventing it from drying out, even after hours of cooking. One caution: don't be tempted to remove the lid during cooking; it can take up to 30 minutes for the food to return to the correct cooking temperature.

CURRIED CHICKPEA
STEW

preparation time · 20 minutes
cooking time · 8 hours
makes · 4 servings

I like to serve this vegetarian stew over steamed rice or couscous and have warm wedges of naan bread alongside for dunking. Use mild, medium or hot curry powder, depending on your taste for spicy food.

ERIC'S OPTIONS

Substitute another canned legume, such as white kidney beans or black beans, for the chickpeas. One or two ribs of celery, halved lengthwise and sliced, can be used instead of zucchini if you prefer its flavor or if that's what you have on hand. Instead of canned diced tomatoes, use 2–3 ripe, medium fresh tomatoes, finely chopped.

1	medium onion, halved and sliced	1
1	medium carrot, halved lengthwise and chopped	1
1	medium zucchini, cubed	1
2	garlic cloves, chopped	2
1 Tbsp	curry powder	15 mL
2 cups	vegetable stock	500 mL
1	14 oz (398 mL) can diced tomatoes	1
1	19 oz (540 mL) can chickpeas, drained and rinsed	1
½ tsp	sugar	2 mL
to taste	salt	to taste
2 Tbsp	chopped fresh cilantro, mint or parsley	30 mL

Combine all the ingredients except the fresh herbs in your slow cooker. Cover and cook on the low setting for 8 hours. Before serving, stir in the fresh herbs, taste for seasoning and add more salt, if needed.

ALMOST BAKED BEANS

preparation time · 20 minutes
cooking time · 8 hours 45 minutes
makes · 6 servings

These are "almost baked beans" because after 8 hours in the slow cooker, they almost taste like oven-baked beans. Boil the beans the night before to get a quick start on the dish the next morning.

ERIC'S OPTIONS
Instead of ham, use cubes of smoked turkey. Make this a vegetarian dish by omitting the ham and using vegetable stock instead of chicken stock.

2 cups	dried white or navy beans	500 mL
1 cup	ketchup	250 mL
1 cup	barbecue sauce	250 mL
1 cup	chicken stock	250 mL
¼ cup	molasses	60 mL
¼ cup	packed golden brown sugar	60 mL
1	large onion, chopped	1
1 Tbsp	Dijon mustard	15 mL
1 ½ cups	cubed ham	375 mL

Place the beans in a pot and cover with 3–4 inches (8–10 cm) of cold water. Bring to a boil, and then reduce the heat to a gentle simmer. Cook until the beans are just tender, but still slightly firm to the bite, about 45 minutes. Drain well. (If you're cooking the beans the night before, cool to room temperature, cover and store in the refrigerator.)

Place the beans and all the remaining ingredients in the slow cooker and mix well. Cover and cook on the low setting for 8 hours.

NO CHOPPING REQUIRED
BEEF CHILI

preparation time	·	5 minutes
cooking time	·	8 hours 5 minutes
makes	·	4 servings

If you're in a big hurry or your knife skills aren't great, this delicious chili is designed for you.

ERIC'S OPTIONS
Top each bowl of chili with a dollop of sour cream and/or grated Monterey Jack or cheddar cheese. Substitute an equal amount of ground pork or turkey for the beef.

1 lb	lean ground beef	500 g
2 cups	bottled salsa	500 mL
1	14 oz (398 mL) can crushed tomatoes	1
1	14 oz (398 mL) can diced tomatoes	1
1 cup	vegetable juice cocktail	250 mL
1	19 oz (540 mL) can red or white kidney beans, drained and rinsed	1
2 tsp	chili powder	10 mL
1 tsp	ground cumin	5 mL
1 cup	frozen corn kernels	250 mL

Brown the beef in a pot over medium heat, stirring to break it up, until it's cooked through and no pink is showing, about 5 minutes. Drain the fat off and place the meat in the slow cooker. Mix in all the remaining ingredients. Cover and cook on the low setting for 8 hours. Ladle the chili into bowls and serve.

VEGETARIAN BLACK BEAN CHILI

preparation time · 20 minutes
cooking time · 8 hours
makes · 6 servings

Here's a pleasingly spiced, Southwest-style chili; serve it with tortilla chips for dunking.

ERIC'S OPTIONS
Top bowls of the chili with a dollop of sour cream and/or grated Monterey Jack or cheddar cheese. Make the chili with another type of bean, such as red or white kidney beans or pinto beans. For a spicy, smoky-tasting chili, add 1–2 chipotle peppers (available in cans at most supermarkets), finely chopped.

1	28 oz (796 mL) can crushed tomatoes	1
1	28 oz (796 mL) can diced tomatoes	1
1 cup	beer or vegetable stock	250 mL
1	medium onion, finely chopped	1
1	medium green bell pepper, finely chopped	1
2	19 oz (540 mL) cans black beans, drained and rinsed	2
1 cup	frozen corn kernels	250 mL
1–2 tsp	hot pepper sauce, such as Tabasco	5–10 mL
2 tsp	chili powder	10 mL
1 tsp	ground cumin	5 mL
1 tsp	dried oregano	5 mL
to taste	salt and freshly ground black pepper	to taste
¼ cup	chopped fresh cilantro	60 mL

Place all the ingredients except the cilantro in your slow cooker. Cover and cook on the low setting for 8 hours. To serve, stir in the cilantro, taste for seasoning and add more salt and pepper if needed.

ABOUT BLACK BEANS

Black beans, also called turtle beans, are earthy, somewhat sweet-tasting, black-skinned legumes with cream-colored flesh. They're a staple ingredient in South and Central America and parts of the Caribbean, such as Cuba. In North America you'll see them used in a variety of dishes, such as soup, salad and salsa. A good source of fiber and protein, they're available dried and also fully cooked in cans. When using canned black beans, reduce the sodium content by gently rinsing the beans in cold water and draining them well before using.

CHICKEN COCONUT
CURRY

preparation time · 25 minutes
cooking time · 8 hours 10 minutes
makes · 4 servings

Serve this curry with steamed basmati rice, chutney, yogurt and pappadums, a crisp, cracker-like bread sold in the Asian-foods aisle of most supermarkets.

ERIC'S OPTIONS
Substitute cubed turkey thighs or pork tenderloin for the chicken thighs. Reduce the calorie and fat content by using light coconut milk.

2 Tbsp	vegetable oil	30 mL
1 lb	boneless, skinless chicken thighs, cubed	500 g
1 Tbsp	cornstarch	15 mL
3	medium red potatoes, cubed	3
1	medium onion, halved and sliced	1
1	28 oz (796 mL) can diced tomatoes	1
1	14 oz (398 mL) can coconut milk	1
1 cup	chicken stock	250 mL
1–2 Tbsp	curry powder	15–30 mL
to taste	salt	to taste
24	snow or snap peas, blanched (see How to Blanch Vegetables, page 32)	24

Heat the oil in a large skillet over medium-high heat. Coat the chicken with the cornstarch, add to the skillet and brown on all sides. Place the browned chicken, potatoes, onion, tomatoes, coconut milk, stock and curry powder in the slow cooker and stir to combine. Cover and cook on the low setting for 8 hours. When ready to serve, season with salt and stir in the blanched peas; they'll heat through in 1–2 minutes.

SLOW COOKER PORK BACK RIBS
in BARBECUE SAUCE

preparation time · 20 minutes
cooking time · 8 hours plus grilling time
makes · 4–6 servings

To quickly get the ribs cooking in the morning, trim and grill them the night before, cool to room temperature and refrigerate overnight. Serve the ribs with Quick Coleslaw with Apples, Raisins and Pecans (page 166) and Roasted Potato Wedges with Chili and Parmesan (page 178).

ERIC'S OPTIONS
Replace the pork back ribs with 2½ lb (1.25 kg) of pork side ribs, well trimmed and cut into 2- to 3-rib portions.

2 Tbsp	chili powder	30 mL
1 Tbsp	ground cumin	15 mL
½ tsp	cayenne pepper	2 mL
½ tsp	salt	2 mL
3	medium-sized racks pork back ribs, trimmed of excess fat and cut into 2- to 3-rib portions	3
1¾ cups	barbecue sauce	425 mL
1 cup	beer or chicken stock	250 mL
½ cup	apple juice	125 mL
2 Tbsp	apple cider vinegar	30 mL
2 Tbsp	honey	30 mL

Preheat an indoor or outdoor grill to medium-high. Combine the chili powder, cumin, cayenne and salt in a small bowl; rub the mixture on the ribs. Lightly oil the bars of your grill and cook the ribs for 3–4 minutes per side, or until nicely seared but not cooked through.

Place the ribs in the slow cooker. Combine the remaining ingredients in a bowl and pour over the ribs. Cover and cook on the low setting for 8 hours.

ABOUT PORK RIBS

The 2 main types of pork ribs available for sale are back ribs and side ribs, also called spare ribs. Back ribs are cut from the pork loin, the same portion of the pig that pork chops come from. These ribs are fairly lean and have a generous amount of meat between the bones, which explains why they're more costly.

Side ribs are taken from the side (belly) of the animal. They contain more bone than meat and are fairly fatty and should be trimmed well before cooking. However, cooks are attracted to side ribs because they know that the bones and fat enhance the flavor of the meat as it cooks. St. Louis–style ribs are pork side ribs with the brisket bone removed. This creates a long, even rack of ribs popular for slow cooking on the barbecue.

TURKEY and VEGETABLE STEW

preparation time · 20 minutes
cooking time · 8 hours 5 minutes
makes · 4 servings

The peas added at the end of cooking make a fresh contrast to the slow-cooked meat and vegetables in their tasty sauce. Serve this homey stew on a bed of egg noodles, steamed rice or Garlic Mashed Yukon Gold Potatoes (page 176).

ERIC'S OPTIONS
Substitute boneless, skinless chicken breast or thigh for the turkey. Give the stew a richer taste by using whipping (heavy) cream instead of light cream. Instead of peas, try frozen green beans or kernel corn.

1 ¼ lb	boneless, skinless turkey breast or thigh, cubed	625 g
2	medium carrots, halved lengthwise and chopped	2
2	celery ribs, halved lengthwise and chopped	2
1	medium onion, halved and sliced	1
1 tsp	dried thyme	5 mL
2	garlic cloves, minced	2
2 ½ cups	chicken stock	625 mL
¼ cup	all-purpose flour	60 mL
⅓ cup	light cream	75 mL
½ cup	frozen peas	125 mL
to taste	salt and white pepper	to taste

Place the turkey, carrot, celery, onion, thyme and garlic in the slow cooker. Whisk the stock and flour in a bowl until well combined. Add to the slow cooker and mix well. Cover and cook on the low setting for 8 hours.

Stir in the cream, peas, salt and pepper; cover and cook for another 5 minutes, or until the peas are heated through.

MEATBALLS
in MARINARA SAUCE

preparation time ·	10 minutes	
cooking time ·	8 hours	
makes ·	4 servings	

Serve these tangy meatballs over hot pasta with a fresh salad alongside. Or make open-faced sandwiches by serving the meatballs on thick slices of toasted garlic bread.

ERIC'S OPTIONS
To increase your vegetable intake, add 1 rib of celery, sliced in half lengthwise and chopped, 1 small green bell pepper, chopped, ½ medium onion, chopped, and 1 small carrot, grated, to the slow cooker with the other ingredients.

24–32	frozen (do not thaw) store-bought or homemade meatballs (see Large Batch Roast and Freeze Meatballs, page 159)	24–32
1	28 oz (796 mL) can crushed tomatoes	1
1	28 oz (796 mL) can diced tomatoes	1
½ cup	beef stock or red wine	125 mL
1 tsp	dried oregano	5 mL
1 tsp	dried basil	5 mL
½ tsp	sugar	2 mL
to taste	salt and freshly ground black pepper	to taste

Place all the ingredients in the slow cooker and stir to combine. Cover and cook on the low setting for 8 hours.

CASUAL FAMILY FARE

CHAPTER SIX

NO-FUSS VEGETARIAN BAKED BEANS

preparation time · 15 minutes
cooking time · 60 minutes
makes · 6 servings

I call these no-fuss baked beans because canned beans are used, rather than dried beans. This reduces the cooking time by at least 2 hours. If you mix all the ingredients together in the morning or the night before, you can get the beans in the oven and on the table in 1 hour.

ERIC'S OPTIONS
If you're a meat eater, add 1 cup (250 mL) of cubed ham or Canadian bacon to the beans before you bake them.

1	medium onion, chopped	1
1	14 oz (398 mL) can tomato sauce	1
1 cup	vegetable stock or beer	250 mL
½ cup	barbecue sauce	125 mL
¼ cup	maple syrup	60 mL
2 Tbsp	molasses	30 mL
1 Tbsp	Dijon mustard	15 mL
2 tsp	Worcestershire sauce	10 mL
1	bay leaf	1
3	14 oz (398 mL) cans of great northern or white kidney beans, drained well	3
to taste	salt and freshly ground black pepper	to taste

Preheat the oven to 350°F (180°C). Place all the ingredients in an ovenproof pot and stir to combine. Cover and bake for 60 minutes. Adjust the seasoning and serve.

SKILLET MAC
and CHEESE

preparation time · 10 minutes
cooking time · 9–12 minutes
makes · 4 servings

Here's a quick stovetop way to make macaroni and cheese and still have the heavenly crust of an oven-baked version. I serve it with whole wheat dinner rolls and a platter filled with raw fresh vegetables, such as celery, carrot and cucumber sticks, broccoli and cauliflower florets and cherry tomatoes.

ERIC'S OPTIONS
To add some protein to this dish, mix in a can (6 oz/170 g) of chunk tuna, drained well and coarsely flaked, or 1½ cups (375 mL) of cubed ham or cooked chicken.

2 cups	macaroni	500 mL
2 cups	milk	500 mL
3 Tbsp	all-purpose flour	45 mL
¼ tsp	paprika	1 mL
2 cups	grated cheddar cheese	500 mL
to taste	salt and white pepper	to taste

Bring a large pot of lightly salted water to a boil. Add the macaroni and cook until just tender, about 6–8 minutes. Meanwhile, place the milk, flour and paprika in a bowl and whisk until lump-free. Pour into a 10- to 12-inch (25 to 30 cm) nonstick ovenproof skillet and set over medium heat. Cook the mixture, whisking frequently, until it gently simmers and begins to thicken, about 5 minutes. Mix in 1½ cups (375 mL) of the cheese; season with salt and white pepper. Cook and stir until the cheese melts; reduce to low heat. Place an oven rack 6 inches (15 cm) beneath the broiler; preheat the broiler.

Drain the cooked macaroni well and mix into the cheese sauce. Stir in a little extra milk if you find the consistency too thick. Remove from the heat. Sprinkle the remaining ½ cup (125 mL) of cheese overtop and place under the broiler until it's nicely browned, about 3–4 minutes.

THIN-CRUST TORTILLA PIZZA

preparation time	·	15 minutes
cooking time	·	10–12 minutes
makes	·	1 pizza/2–3 servings

When the pizza craving strikes, you can whip one up in minutes with this simple recipe using tortillas you can find at any grocery store.

ERIC'S OPTIONS
Double or triple this recipe if you're feeding a larger group.

2	10-inch (25 cm) white or whole wheat tortillas	2
1½ cups	grated mozzarella cheese	375 mL
⅓ cup	pizza sauce	75 mL
	your choice of toppings, such as mushrooms, bell peppers, pepperoni, olives and nuggets of goat cheese	

Preheat the oven to 375°F (190°C). Place 1 tortilla on a parchment paper-lined baking sheet. Evenly top with half the grated cheese. Top with the second tortilla. Spread the pizza sauce overtop. Sprinkle with the remaining cheese and your desired pizza toppings. Bake for 10–12 minutes. Cool for a minute or two before cutting into wedges and serving.

CHICKPEA BURGERS

preparation time · 25 minutes
cooking time · 6–8 minutes
makes · 4 servings

If you're not already vegetarian, these delicious, moist, filling, meat-free burgers just may convince you! Serve them with your choice of toppings, such as tomato, cucumber, lettuce and tzatziki sauce.

ERIC'S OPTIONS
These burgers can be formed and coated with the crumbs up to 1 day in advance. Cover and store in the refrigerator until ready to cook.

1	19 oz (540 mL) can chickpeas	1
2 Tbsp	tahini (see Note page 106)	30 mL
1	large egg, beaten	1
⅓ cup	grated onion	75 mL
⅓ cup	grated carrot	75 mL
3 Tbsp	chopped fresh cilantro	45 mL
1 Tbsp	curry powder	15 mL
½ tsp	salt	2 mL
¾ cup	breadcrumbs	175 mL
3 Tbsp	vegetable oil	45 mL
4	hamburger buns	4

Drain the chickpeas, rinse in cold water, and drain well again. Place in a food processor, along with the tahini and egg. Pulse until almost smooth, but still a little coarse in texture. Transfer the mixture to a bowl and mix in the onion, carrot, cilantro, curry powder and salt.

Place the breadcrumbs in a shallow dish. Moisten your hands with cold water and form one-quarter of the mixture (it will be quite moist) into a ¾-inch-thick (2 cm) patty. Coat the patty completely with the breadcrumbs, pressing on the crumbs to help them adhere. Set the coated patty on a separate plate lined with parchment paper. Repeat with the remaining mixture. Cover and refrigerate the patties for 20 minutes to firm them up.

Instructions follow on page 106 ...

Heat the oil in a large nonstick skillet over medium heat. Add the chickpea burgers and cook for 3–4 minutes per side, or until completely heated through. Serve them in the buns with assorted toppings.

NOTE
Tahini is a Middle Eastern-style paste made from ground sesame seeds. You can find it at most supermarkets and delis.

CHICKPEAS: ECONOMICAL AND NUTRITIOUS

Chickpeas, also called garbanzo beans, are the seeds of a plant native to Turkey, but which also flourishes in other parts of the Mediterranean and the Middle East. When people think of chickpeas, they often think of the well-known dip called hummus, but chickpeas are used in a number of other dishes, from salads to soups to stews. Chickpeas are an excellent source of protein, potassium and fiber and contain calcium and vitamin B6. Another good thing about them is that they're much easier to digest than other beans and are less likely to cause flatulence.

HOMEMADE
FISH STICKS

preparation time · 15 minutes
cooking time · 12 minutes
makes · 4 servings

These "real" fish sticks are made with solid pieces of fish, not the small flakes somehow bound together that you find in some store-bought, mass-produced fish sticks. Snapper, basa, cod or haddock are good choices for fish sticks. If you like, serve them with a dip, such as cocktail or tartar sauce.

ERIC'S OPTIONS
For tasty fish burgers, stuff 2 or 3 fish sticks in a bun with lettuce, sliced tomatoes, a sliced dill pickle and tartar sauce.

2 Tbsp	vegetable or olive oil	30 mL
½ cup	breadcrumbs	125 mL
2 tsp	freshly grated lemon zest	10 mL
½ tsp	paprika	2 mL
pinch	cayenne pepper (optional)	pinch
to taste	salt and freshly ground black pepper	to taste
1½ lb	boneless skinless fish fillets	750 g
⅓ cup	mayonnaise	75 mL

Preheat the oven to 400°F (200°C). Line a baking sheet with parchment paper and brush with the oil. Combine the breadcrumbs, lemon zest, paprika, cayenne (if using), salt and pepper in a shallow dish. Cut the fish into pieces approximately 3 inches (8 cm) long and 1 inch (2.5 cm) wide. Brush the fish with a thin layer of mayonnaise. Place 1 piece of fish on the breadcrumb mixture, coat all sides and transfer to the prepared baking sheet. Repeat with the remaining fish. Bake for 8 minutes, turn the fish over and bake for 4 minutes more, or until just cooked through. Serve hot.

FISH
TACOS

preparation time · 20 minutes
cooking time · 15 minutes
makes · 4 servings

Here's a simple, tasty, Mexican-style way to incorporate more nutritious fish into your diet. Use any fish you like, such as halibut, haddock, snapper or salmon.

ERIC'S OPTIONS
Stuff the tacos with any other ingredients that appeal to you, such as thinly sliced bell pepper, chopped red onions or grated Monterey Jack or cheddar cheese. Or use guacamole instead of sliced avocados. To make a quick guacamole, place a medium, peeled avocado and the juice of a lime in a bowl and mash well. Mix in ¼ cup (60 mL) sour cream and ½ cup (125 mL) store-bought salsa.

4	6 oz (175 g) fish fillets	4
2 Tbsp	olive oil	30 mL
2 Tbsp	freshly squeezed lime juice	30 mL
½ tsp	ground cumin	2 mL
½ tsp	chili powder	2 mL
½ tsp	dried oregano	2 mL
pinch	cayenne pepper	pinch
to taste	salt and freshly ground black pepper	to taste
8	taco shells	8
2 cups	shredded head or leaf lettuce	500 mL
1	medium avocado, sliced into wedges	1
1 cup	salsa	250 mL

Instructions follow on page 110 ...

Preheat the oven to 425°F (220°C). Line a baking dish with parchment paper. Place the fish in a single layer in the baking dish. Combine the olive oil, lime juice, cumin, chili powder, oregano, cayenne, salt and pepper in a small bowl, stirring well. Brush or spoon the mixture onto the fish. Bake for 10–12 minutes, or until the fish is just cooked through. Remove from the oven and cool slightly. Meanwhile, heat the taco shells in the oven for a few minutes.

Coarsely flake the fish. Stuff the tacos, dividing the lettuce, avocado, flaked fish and salsa evenly between them. Serve immediately.

WHEN IS FISH COOKED?

Fish is cooked when it turns opaque and the flakes begin to slightly separate. With some fish, such as salmon, a white-colored fat will seep out when the fish is cooked. The fish should feel slightly firm, but not hard, which is a sign you've overcooked it. If it's too soft, it's undercooked. The old fisherman's rule of thumb for cooking time is to allow 10 minutes per inch (2.5 cm) of thickness. This seems to hold true if you're pan-frying or grilling fish over medium to medium-high heat. When baking fish in the oven, though, you need to add a few minutes: the dish you're cooking the fish in will have to reach oven temperature before the fish really starts cooking.

HONEY MUSTARD
CHICKEN LEGS

preparation time · 10 minutes
cooking time · 45–50 minutes
makes · 4 servings

Serve this easy-to-make chicken dish with baked potatoes and steamed broccoli drizzled with a little melted butter and lemon juice.

ERIC'S OPTIONS
You can substitute large, bone-in chicken breasts for the legs. If you like garlic, add a crushed clove to the basting mixture.

4	large whole chicken legs	4
to taste	salt and freshly ground black pepper	to taste
¼ cup	honey, warmed	60 mL
2 Tbsp	Dijon mustard	30 mL
1 Tbsp	freshly squeezed lemon juice	15 mL
1 tsp	dried crumbled sage	5 mL

Preheat the oven to 375°F (190°C). Choose a baking dish large enough to accommodate the chicken in a single layer and line with parchment paper. Place the chicken in the prepared dish and season with salt and pepper. Bake for 20 minutes.

Meanwhile, combine the remaining ingredients in a bowl. When the chicken has roasted for 20 minutes, spoon the honey mixture over the chicken. Bake for another 25–30 minutes, until the chicken is cooked through and nicely glazed. Serve the chicken drizzled with any glaze left in the bottom of the pan.

CHICKEN BURGERS with MUSHROOMS and MOZZARELLA

preparation time · 15 minutes
cooking time · 6-8 minutes
makes · 4 servings

Why opt for a mass-produced, fast-food chicken burger when you can quickly whip up your own tastier version at home and have control of the ingredients used to make it?

ERIC'S OPTIONS

For an additional hit of flavor, spread the chicken breasts with barbecue sauce before topping with the mushrooms and cheese. For Italian-style chicken burgers, spread the chicken with a tomato-based pasta sauce before topping with the mushrooms and cheese. Or substitute grated cheddar, Asiago or provolone for the mozzarella.

3 Tbsp	olive oil	45 mL
½ lb	white or brown mushrooms, sliced	250 g
1	garlic clove, chopped	1
4	5 oz (150 g) boneless, skinless chicken breasts	4
1 tsp	dried oregano	5 mL
½ tsp	paprika	2 mL
to taste	salt and freshly ground black pepper	to taste
4	slices of mozzarella cheese	4
4	hamburger buns	4
3 Tbsp	mayonnaise	45 mL
2 cups	organic mixed salad greens	500 mL

Preheat an indoor or outdoor grill to medium-high. Place 1 Tbsp (15 mL) of the oil in a nonstick skillet over medium heat. When the oil is hot, add the mushrooms and garlic and cook until the mushrooms are tender, about 5 minutes. Remove from the heat and reserve.

Brush the chicken with the remaining 2 Tbsp (30 mL) of oil; season with oregano, paprika, salt and pepper. Grill the chicken for 3–4 minutes per side, or until entirely cooked through and no pink is showing when tested in the thickest portion.

Top each breast with one-quarter of the mushrooms and 1 slice of cheese. If cooking on the barbecue, close the lid and cook until the cheese is melted. If cooking on a stovetop grill pan, cover and cook until the cheese is melted.

Cut the buns in half and spread with the mayonnaise. Place the salad greens on the bottom half, add the chicken and the top half of the bun and serve.

ABOUT WHITE AND BROWN MUSHROOMS

White and brown (also called cremini) mushrooms can be used interchangeably in all sorts of recipes. The 2 mushrooms are related, but white mushrooms, also called button mushrooms, are milder tasting and have a less dense texture than their earthier-tasting cousins. When buying either mushroom, look for firm, unblemished ones that are evenly colored and have tightly closed caps. Refrigerate the mushrooms in the paper bag or plastic container you bought them in. They'll be at their best if used as soon as possible, but they'll keep for few days if they were in prime condition when purchased. Before using mushrooms, wipe them clean with a damp paper towel.

CRISPY OVEN-BAKED
PORK CUTLETS

preparation time · 15 minutes
cooking time · 10–12 minutes
makes · 4 servings

The mayonnaise, which replaces the more common flour and egg coating used to ensure the crumb coating adheres, gives these cutlets a tangy flavor and helps them stay moist. Serve the cutlets with store-bought or homemade applesauce (see McIntosh Apple Sauce, page 181).

ERIC'S OPTIONS
Instead of pork, use turkey or veal cutlets. Plain breadcrumbs can replace the cornflake crumbs.

2 Tbsp	vegetable oil	30 mL
¾ cup	cornflake crumbs	175 mL
½ tsp	ground sage	2 mL
¼ tsp	paprika	1 mL
pinch	cayenne pepper (optional)	pinch
to taste	salt and freshly ground black pepper	to taste
¼ cup	mayonnaise	60 mL
4	5 or 6 oz (150 or 175 g) pork cutlets	4

Preheat the oven to 450°F (230°C). Line a baking sheet with parchment paper and brush with the oil. Combine the cornflake crumbs, sage, paprika, cayenne (if using), salt and pepper in a shallow dish and mix well. Evenly coat each pork cutlet with a thin layer of mayonnaise and place on the crumb mixture. Coat on all sides, gently pressing on the crumbs to help them adhere. Place on the prepared baking sheet. Bake for 5 minutes, then flip the cutlets over and bake for another 5–7 minutes, or until just cooked through, with just a hint of pale pink in the middle.

ROASTED BRATWURST on a BUN with RED ONION RELISH

preparation time · 15 minutes
cooking time · 35–40 minutes
makes · 4 servings

If you make the relish on your day off, you can pop the sausages into the oven and just relax while they're roasting. The relish will keep in the refrigerator for up to 2 weeks if stored in a tightly sealed jar, and it's delicious served on burgers or alongside baked ham or pâté, as well as these sausages.

ERIC'S OPTIONS
Use other types of sausages, such as turkey, weisswurst or European-style wieners. For a spicy and sweet taste, top the sausages with Dijon mustard before spooning on the relish.

2 Tbsp	vegetable oil	30 mL
2 cups	halved and thinly sliced red onion (about 1 large onion)	500 mL
¼ cup	packed golden brown sugar	60 mL
¼ cup	balsamic vinegar	60 mL
1 tsp	chopped fresh rosemary	5 mL
¼ cup	currants	60 mL
to taste	salt and freshly ground black pepper	to taste
4	bratwurst sausages	4
4	hot dog buns, warmed	4

Heat the oil in a pot over medium heat. Add the onion and cook, stirring, until very tender and almost sticky, about 10 minutes. Stir in the sugar, vinegar, rosemary, currants, salt and pepper. Bring the mixture to a gentle simmer and cook until it thickens and becomes almost syrupy, about 5 minutes. Cool to room temperature; if making ahead, store in the refrigerator until needed.

Preheat the oven to 375°F (190°C). Line an ovenproof dish with parchment paper. Place the sausages in the prepared dish and roast, turning once, until golden and cooked through, about 20–25 minutes. Place the sausages in the buns, top with a generous spoonful of the relish and enjoy.

SLOPPY JOE–STUFFED BAKED POTATOES

preparation time · 15 minutes
cooking time · 50–60 minutes
makes · 4 servings

This twist on the traditional Sloppy Joe replaces the bun with a hot baked potato. Healthy and delicious! Try serving these with Family-Style Salad with Bacon Ranch Dressing (page 164).

ERIC'S OPTIONS
Substitute ground turkey for the beef.

4	medium baking potatoes	4
¾ lb	lean ground beef	375 g
½	medium onion, finely chopped	½
1	14 oz (398 mL) can tomato sauce	1
⅓ cup	barbecue sauce	75 mL
¼ cup	water	60 mL
1 tsp	ground cumin	5 mL
½ tsp	chili powder	2 mL
to taste	salt and freshly ground black pepper to taste	to taste
½–1 cup	grated cheddar, mozzarella or Jack cheese	125–250 mL
2	green onions, finely chopped	2

Preheat the oven to 350°F (180°C). Wash and dry the potatoes, and prick them several times with a fork. Bake until tender, about 50–60 minutes.

Meanwhile, brown the beef and onion in a large, nonstick skillet over medium heat. Cook, stirring to break up the meat, until the beef is cooked through and no longer pink, about 5 minutes. Drain off the excess fat. Add the tomato sauce, barbecue sauce, water, cumin, chili powder, salt and pepper. Bring the mixture to a gentle simmer and cook for 15 minutes. (If it gets too thick, add a bit more water.)

Make a slit down the middle of the cooked potatoes and squeeze them open to expose the flesh. Top with a generous amount of the Sloppy Joe mixture. Sprinkle with the cheese and green onions and serve immediately.

PAN-SEARED STEAKS
with ONION GRAVY

preparation time · 15 minutes
cooking time · about 15 minutes
makes · 4 servings

Complete this comforting steak and gravy dish with boiled small new potatoes, a steamed green vegetable such as beans, asparagus or broccoli, and Mini-Carrots with Honey, Ginger and Lemon (page 173).

ERIC'S OPTIONS
If you like veal, substitute four 6 oz (175 g) veal cutlets for the steaks.

2 Tbsp	vegetable oil	30 mL
1½ lb	sirloin or round steak, cut into 4 portions	750 g
to taste	salt and freshly ground black pepper	to taste
1	large onion, halved and sliced	1
2 Tbsp	all-purpose flour	30 mL
1½ tsp	minced fresh thyme, or ½ tsp (2 mL) dried	7 mL
1½ cups	beef stock	375 mL

Heat the oil in a large skillet over medium-high heat. Season the steaks with salt and pepper and sear for 2–3 minutes per side (cook 1 minute per side longer if you like them more well done). Transfer to a plate.

Add the onion to the skillet and cook until tender, about 5 minutes. Mix in the flour and thyme until well combined. Slowly, stirring steadily, pour in the stock. Bring the mixture to a simmer and cook until slightly thickened; season with salt and pepper. Return the steaks to the pan and heat through for a few minutes before serving.

CHICKEN-FRIED STEAK
with PAN GRAVY

preparation time · 15 minutes
cooking time · about 10 minutes
makes · 4 servings

Here's a Texas-style way to tastily coat and fry tenderized beefsteaks. It's called chicken-fried steak because the coating is similar to the one used for fried chicken. Mashed potatoes are a traditional accompaniment, and I also like to serve it with buttered green beans and kernel corn.

ERIC'S OPTIONS
For a richer, tangy-tasting gravy, replace ¼ cup (60 mL) of the milk with the same amount of sour cream.

1	large egg	1
1¾ cups	milk	425 mL
1 cup	all-purpose flour	250 mL
½ tsp	salt	2 mL
½ tsp	freshly ground black pepper	2 mL
½ tsp	ground sage	2 mL
¼ tsp	paprika	1 mL
4	5 to 6 oz (150 to 175 g) tenderized beef steaks	4
	vegetable oil	

Preheat the oven to 200°F (95°C). Line a baking sheet with parchment paper. Beat the egg and ¼ cup (60 mL) of the milk together in a bowl. Combine the flour, salt, pepper, sage and paprika in a shallow dish, mixing well. Coat each steak with the flour and then dip in the egg mixture. Coat in flour again and place on the prepared baking sheet. Set the leftover flour aside.

Place a very large skillet over medium-high heat and add enough oil to form a layer ¼ inch (6 mm) deep. When the oil is hot, add the steaks and fry until golden brown and cooked through, about 3 minutes per side. Drain on paper towels and place in the oven to keep warm.

Drain all but about 2 Tbsp (30 mL) of the oil from the skillet. Stir in 2 Tbsp (30 mL) of the reserved flour until well combined. Continue cooking over medium heat until the mixture is light brown, about 2–3 minutes. Slowly whisk in the remaining 1½ cups (375 mL) of milk and bring to a simmer. Cook for a few minutes until the gravy thickens (add a little more milk if it becomes too thick); season with salt and pepper. Serve the steaks on individual plates, topped with the gravy.

ALL-DRESSED
POTATO SKINS

preparation time ·	25 minutes	
cooking time ·	about 1 hour 15 minutes	
makes ·	4–6 servings	

These are tender baked potatoes cut into wedges and topped with savory ingredients the whole family will enjoy. For a meal, serve with mixed greens or Caesar salad. To speed up preparation, bake the potatoes on a day off, cool to room temperature and store in the refrigerator so they will be ready to cut into wedges and top for a quick midweek meal.

ERIC'S OPTIONS
Make Tex-Mex potato skins by using Monterey Jack cheese instead of cheddar and chopped cilantro instead of green onions. Top the sour cream with a touch of salsa.

4	medium baking potatoes	4
to taste	seasoning salt	to taste
1½	cups grated cheddar cheese	375 mL
6	strips of bacon, diced, cooked until crispy and drained well	6
1 cup	sour cream	250 mL
3	green onions, finely chopped	3

Preheat the oven to 350°F (180°C). Wash and dry the potatoes, and prick them several times with a fork. Bake until tender, about 50–60 minutes. Let them cool.

Line a baking sheet with parchment paper. Cut each baked potato in half lengthwise. Scoop out enough of the potato flesh (keep it for another meal like hash browns) to leave a half-inch (1 cm) thick shell of skin and flesh. Cut each half potato lengthwise into 3 wedges and place skin-side down on the baking sheet. Sprinkle the potatoes with the seasoning salt and top with the cheese and bacon. Bake in the preheated oven for 12 to 15 minutes, until the cheese is melted and the potatoes are heated through. Arrange the potato skins on a platter. Top each with a small dollop of sour cream and sprinkle with green onions. Set on the dining room table and devour.

QUICK MEALS FROM AROUND THE WORLD

CHAPTER SEVEN

SHRIMP, SNOW PEAS, MUSHROOMS and TOFU in MISO BROTH

preparation time	20 minutes
cooking time	about 10 minutes
makes	4 servings

This is like a chunky version of miso soup. Instead of just a few token garnishes, this hearty broth is packed with tastes and textures: succulent shrimp, crisp snow peas, earthy mushrooms and tender tofu.

ERIC'S OPTIONS
Instead of medium to large shrimp, use ⅓ cup (75 mL) of small, cooked salad shrimp. To make it more Japanese-style, use sliced fresh shiitake mushrooms, stems removed, instead of white or brown mushrooms.

4 cups	chicken or vegetable stock	1 L
1	garlic clove, finely chopped	1
2 tsp	grated fresh ginger	10 mL
1 Tbsp	soy sauce	15 mL
pinch	crushed chili flakes	pinch
4–6	white or brown mushrooms, thinly sliced	4–6
3 Tbsp	shiro (white) miso (see Using Miso page 126)	45 mL
18	snow peas, trimmed and sliced	18
20	cooked, peeled, medium to large shrimp (see Note)	20
1	10 oz (300 g) package soft tofu, cut in ½-inch (1 cm) cubes	1
2	green onions, thinly sliced	2

Combine the stock, garlic, ginger, soy sauce, chili flakes and mushrooms in a medium pot. Bring to a boil over high heat. Reduce the heat to a gentle simmer; simmer for 5 minutes. Add the miso and stir until it dissolves. Add the snow peas, shrimp and tofu. Return to a simmer and cook for another 1–2 minutes; do not boil. Ladle the soup into bowls, sprinkle with the green onions and serve.

NOTE
Cooked, peeled shrimp are sold at almost every supermarket. If you've bought them frozen, thaw them and pat them dry with a paper towel before adding them to the soup.

USING MISO

Miso, also called bean paste, comes in a variety of styles, from light to dark in color, to mild and pungent in flavor. For soup, shiro miso, also called white miso, even though it's more yellow in color, is a good choice. It is milder tasting and not overly salty, and will add a nice base flavor to the broth, but won't overpower the other ingredients in the soup. Miso is sold at Japanese food stores, Asian markets and some supermarkets.

BEAN and
TURKEY ENCHILADAS

	preparation time	20 minutes
	cooking time	20–25 minutes
	makes	4 servings

Here's a Mexican-style way to use those leftovers from a Thanksgiving, Christmas or Sunday roast turkey dinner. For a side dish, serve Grilled Corn with Lime and Cumin (page 169).

ERIC'S OPTIONS
Substitute cooked and shredded chicken, pork or beef for the turkey.

1	14 oz (398 mL) can tomato sauce	1
1 tsp	chili powder	5 mL
½ tsp	ground cumin	2 mL
to taste	hot pepper sauce, such as Tabasco	to taste
4	10-inch (25 cm) tortillas	4
1	14 oz (398 mL) can refried beans	1
2 cups	shredded, cooked turkey	500 mL
1½ cups	grated Monterey Jack or cheddar cheese	375 mL
1	large, fresh jalapeño pepper, thinly sliced (optional)	1

Preheat the oven to 375°F (190°C). Line a baking sheet with parchment paper. Combine the tomato sauce, chili powder, cumin and hot pepper sauce in a bowl. Place the tortillas on your work surface and spread an equal amount of the refried beans down the center of each.

Top the beans with the turkey. Drizzle 1½ Tbsp (22.5 mL) of the sauce over the turkey on each tortilla. Roll the tortillas into cylinders and place on the baking sheet, spacing them about 2 inches (5 cm) apart. Spoon the remaining sauce evenly over the tortillas and sprinkle with the cheese. Top each enchilada, if desired, with a few thin slices of jalapeño pepper. Bake for 20–25 minutes, or until heated through and the cheese is melted.

SHRIMP and VEGETABLE FAJITAS

preparation time — 25 minutes
cooking time — about 5 minutes
makes — 4 servings (2 fajitas each)

Stuffing your own warm tortillas with shrimp and sizzling-hot vegetables at the table is a fun and relaxed way to dine.

ERIC'S OPTIONS
If you like things spicy, add 1–2 Tbsp (15–30 mL) of chopped fresh or canned jalapeño peppers to the vegetable mixture when sautéing. Instead of Monterey Jack, use grated cheddar cheese if that's what you have on hand or prefer.

2 Tbsp	vegetable oil	30 mL
1	medium onion, halved and thinly sliced	1
1 each	medium red, green and yellow bell pepper, halved and thinly sliced	1 each
1 tsp	chili powder	5 mL
½ tsp	ground cumin	2 mL
to taste	salt and hot pepper sauce, such as Tabasco	to taste
32	cooked, peeled medium shrimp, tails removed	32
1½ cups	grated Monterey Jack cheese	375 mL
2 cups	shredded head or leaf lettuce	500 mL
1 cup	salsa, or to taste	250 mL
8	10-inch (25 cm) tortillas, warmed	8

Heat the oil in a large, nonstick skillet over medium-high heat. Add the onion and bell peppers and cook, stirring, for 2 minutes. Mix in the chili powder, cumin, salt and hot pepper sauce. Toss in the shrimp and cook for 2–3 minutes more, or until the shrimp are just heated through.

Spoon the mixture into a serving bowl and place on the table. Set out the cheese, lettuce, salsa and tortillas alongside, and invite diners to stuff and roll their own fajitas.

PAN-SEARED TOFU with BABY BOK CHOY and CURRY SAUCE

preparation time	10 minutes
cooking time	6–7 minutes
makes	4 servings

Nutrient-rich tofu and bok choy are accented with a flavorful, easily made sauce. Use mild, medium or hot curry paste according to your palate.

ERIC'S OPTIONS

If you enjoy green Thai curry, use green Thai curry paste instead of the Indian-style curry paste. (See Note) To make this lower in calories and saturated fat, use light coconut milk instead of regular.

1	1 lb (500 g) package firm tofu (see Note)	1
2 Tbsp	vegetable oil	30 mL
8	baby bok choy, washed well and trimmed	8
1	14 oz (398 mL) can coconut milk	1
1 tsp	cornstarch	5 mL
1 Tbsp	Indian-style curry paste (see Note)	15 mL
2 Tbsp	freshly squeezed lime juice	30 mL
2 Tbsp	brown sugar	30 mL
2 tsp	chopped fresh ginger	10 mL
to taste	salt	to taste

Preheat the oven to 200°F (95°C). Drain the tofu well and cut it into 8 slices. Carefully pat the slices dry with paper towel. Heat the oil in a large nonstick skillet over medium-high heat. Add the tofu and sear for 1 minute on each side. Transfer the tofu to a large platter and place in the oven.

Drain the excess oil from the skillet and add ¼ cup (60 mL) of water. Add the bok choy to the skillet, cover and steam for 1 minute. Arrange the bok choy on the platter with the tofu. Add the remaining ingredients to the skillet and whisk to combine. Bring to a boil and cook for 2 minutes. Pour the sauce over the tofu and bok choy and serve.

NOTE

Curry paste is sold in the Asian foods aisle of most supermarkets and at Asian markets. See About Curry Paste (page 63). As for tofu, package sizes can vary from brand to brand. Don't worry about the exact weight as specified in this recipe.

CURRY ALMOND CHICKEN

preparation time 5 minutes
cooking time 45–50 minutes
makes 4 servings

This simple recipe uses just 4 ingredients, but it's full of flavor. For a quick supper, serve it with a green salad or steamed rice and Green Bean Stir-Fry (page 170).

ERIC'S OPTIONS
Substitute 24 chicken wingettes and/or drumettes for the legs. Reduce the baking time to 25–35 minutes. For crispier wings, broil them for a minute or two after baking.

1 cup	ground almonds	250 mL
¼ cup	Indian-style curry paste, (see About Curry Paste page 63)	60 mL
2 Tbsp	freshly squeezed lime juice	30 mL
4	large whole chicken legs	4

Preheat the oven to 375°F (190°C). Line a baking sheet with parchment paper. Spread the ground almonds on a large plate. Combine the curry paste and lime juice in a medium-sized bowl. Add the chicken legs and use your hands or a brush to spread the mixture over all the surfaces of the chicken. Coat the chicken legs with ground almonds, gently pressing to help adhere. Place the chicken on the prepared baking sheet. Bake for 45–50 minutes, or until cooked through and the juice from the chicken is clear, with no signs of pink.

NUTRITIONALLY RICH ALMONDS

Almonds are increasingly popular as snacks on their own or as ingredients in recipes. This makes sense because they not only taste good, but also have the bonus of being very good for you. An excellent source of vitamin E and a good source of fiber, they also contain, among other things, protein, potassium, calcium and iron. Ground almonds are sold at most supermarkets in bags or in bulk; 1 cup (250 mL) weighs about 3½ oz (100 g).

GREEN THAI CURRY CHICKEN

preparation time — 20 minutes
cooking time — about 10 minutes
makes — 4 servings

Serve this addictive, mildly spiced curry on a bed of fragrant, steamed jasmine rice.

ERIC'S OPTIONS
Use an equal amount of sliced, boneless, skinless turkey breast or thigh instead of chicken. Or make Green Thai Curry Shrimp by replacing the chicken with 20–24 raw, peeled, medium to large shrimp. Add them to the curry after bringing the coconut milk to a simmer. Simmer the shrimp until just cooked through, about 3–4 minutes.

3 Tbsp	vegetable oil	45 mL
1	medium onion, halved and sliced	1
1	small red bell pepper, cubed	1
1	garlic clove, chopped	1
1 Tbsp	green Thai curry paste (see Note)	15 mL
1	14 oz (398 mL) can coconut milk	1
¼ cup	water	60 mL
1 lb	boneless, skinless chicken breast or thigh, sliced	500 g
1	14 oz (398 mL) can cut young corn, drained well (see Note, page 67)	1
1	8 oz (224 mL) can sliced bamboo shoots, drained well	1
¼ cup	chopped fresh cilantro or basil	60 mL

Heat 2 Tbsp (30 mL) of the oil in a wok or large skillet over medium-high heat. Add the onion, red pepper and garlic and cook for 2 minutes. Add the curry paste and cook 1 minute more. Add the coconut milk, water, chicken, corn and bamboo shoots and bring to a simmer. Cook for 6–7 minutes, or until the chicken is cooked through. Stir in the cilantro or basil and serve.

NOTE
Green Thai curry paste is sold at Asian markets and in the Asian foods aisle of most supermarkets. See About Curry Paste (page 63).

BAKED FISH with
SWEET CHILI CITRUS GLAZE

preparation time	10 minutes
cooking time	12–15 minutes
makes	4 servings

Those who have tried this recipe report that it's one of their favorites, delivering a lot of flavor with very little effort. Serve the fish with stir-fried baby bok choy and steamed rice or Asian noodles.

ERIC'S OPTIONS
Give the fish a crunchy finish by sprinkling each fillet with ½ tsp (2 mL) of sesame seeds before baking. If you prefer, sprinkle 2–3 Tbsp (30–45 mL) of chopped cilantro on the fish instead of green onions.

4	6 oz (175 g) fish fillets, such as salmon, halibut or snapper	4
to taste	salt	to taste
½ tsp	finely grated orange zest	2 mL
½ tsp	finely grated lemon zest	2 mL
½ tsp	finely grated lime zest	2 mL
2 Tbsp	freshly squeezed orange juice	30 mL
1 Tbsp	freshly squeezed lemon juice	15 mL
1 Tbsp	freshly squeezed lime juice	15 mL
⅓ cup	Thai-style sweet chili sauce (see Note)	75 mL
2	green onions, chopped	2

Preheat the oven to 425°F (220°C). Line a baking dish with parchment paper and add the fish in a single layer; season with salt. Combine all the zest and juice with the chili sauce in a small bowl; spoon over the fish. Bake for 12–15 minutes, or until the fish is cooked through (see When Is Fish Cooked?, page 110). Serve the fish on individual plates, with the pan juices spooned overtop and sprinkled with green onions.

NOTE
Sweet and mildy spicy Thai-style sweet chili sauce is sold at Asian markets and in the Asian foods aisle of most supermarkets.

Baked Fish with Sweet Chili Citrus Glaze

HOW TO BUY AND STORE FRESH FISH

Cookbooks and food professionals—including myself—recommend smelling fish before buying it. The aroma should be sweet and sea-like if it's very fresh. If it smells strongly fishy or has hints of ammonia, the fish is past its prime and should be avoided.

The only problem is that many people are shy about asking the vendor if they can sniff the fish. And, of course, in many supermarkets fish is prepackaged, so you can't smell it anyway. If that's the case, what can you do to ensure that what you're buying is fresh?

Well, start by buying fish from a vendor who sells a lot of seafood; that ensures there's a constant turnover. Ask the fishmonger what's fresh; a reputable seller will point you in the right direction. Take a good, keen look at the fish. Very fresh fish fillets and steaks will have firm flesh that glistens. If it's dull and looks like it's falling apart, the fish has been sitting around too long. When buying whole fish, the eyes should be bright and clear, the skin should be shiny and the body of the fish should look firm, not sunken.

It's best to buy fish the day you'll be cooking it. But if it's very fresh, you can store it in the coldest part of your refrigerator for a day or two.

ASIAN-STYLE PORK CHOP SUPPER

preparation time	15 minutes
cooking time	about 15 minutes
makes	4 servings

This is a complete meal with no fuss: juicy pork chops with sweet chili sauce, broccoli and steamed rice.

ERIC'S OPTIONS
Instead of pork chops, make this dish with four 5–6 oz (100–150 g) boneless, skinless chicken breasts or eight 2–3 oz (50–75 g), boneless skinless chicken thighs. Cooking time and technique remain the same.

1 cup	long-grain white rice	250 mL
2 Tbsp	vegetable oil	30 mL
8	3 oz (75 g) boneless pork loin chops	8
to taste	salt	to taste
¾ cup	Thai-style sweet chili sauce (see Note, page 133)	175 mL
2 Tbsp	freshly squeezed lime juice	30 mL
2 cups	small broccoli florets, blanched (see How to Blanch Vegetables, page 32)	500 mL

Place the rice in a small pot with 1½ cups (375 mL) cold water. Bring to a boil, reduce the heat to its lowest setting, cover and cook until the rice is tender, about 15 minutes.

Meanwhile, heat the oil in a large skillet over medium-high heat. Season the pork with salt and cook it for 3–4 minutes per side, or until just cooked through with only a hint of pale pink in the center. Drain the excess fat from the pan. Add the chili sauce, lime juice and broccoli. Bring to a simmer and cook for 3–4 minutes, turning the pork and broccoli from time to time, until the pork is nicely glazed and the broccoli is heated through. Serve with the steamed rice.

COOKING LONG-GRAIN WHITE RICE

Many home cooks struggle with preparing a pot of perfectly cooked long-grain white rice. Confusion about the ratio of rice to water seems to be the main problem. On the back of a package of long-grain white rice, most companies call for a ratio of 2 parts water to 1 part rice, but I find this produces overcooked, mushy rice. I use a ratio of 1½ parts water to 1 part rice, which creates tender rice that still allows some resistance to the bite. To prepare the rice, rinse it well in cold water and drain it in a sieve. Place the rice and water in the pot and bring it to a boil over high heat. As soon as it boils, reduce the heat to its lowest setting, cover and cook for 15 minutes, or until just tender.

GINGER BEEF

preparation time · 20 minutes
cooking time · about 10 minutes
makes · 4 servings

Here's my ginger-laced version of a dish popular in Chinese restaurants. This dish cooks up quickly, so be prepared: have all the ingredients chopped before you fire up the stove. Serve it with a bowl of steamed rice.

ERIC'S OPTIONS
Use 1 large bunch of gai lan (Chinese broccoli), washed, trimmed and chopped, instead of broccoli florets. Make ginger pork by replacing the beef with 1 lb (500 g) of thinly sliced pork tenderloin. Cooking time and technique remain the same.

1 lb	stir-fry beef (see Note)	500 g
1 Tbsp	chopped fresh ginger	15 mL
2	garlic cloves, chopped	2
3 Tbsp	soy sauce	45 mL
2 tsp	cornstarch	10 mL
3 Tbsp	vegetable oil	45 mL
1	medium onion, halved and sliced	1
4 cups	small broccoli florets	1 L
1 Tbsp	brown sugar	15 mL
1 Tbsp	rice vinegar	15 mL
¼ cup	ketchup	60 mL
½ cup	beef stock	125 mL

Place the beef in a medium bowl. Add the ginger, garlic, soy sauce and cornstarch and toss to coat. Heat 2 Tbsp (30 mL) of the oil in a large skillet or wok over medium-high heat. Add the beef and stir-fry until nicely seared, about 3–4 minutes. Transfer to a bowl. Add the remaining 1 Tbsp (15 mL) of oil to the skillet or wok. Add the onion and broccoli and stir-fry for 2–3 minutes. Stir in the brown sugar, vinegar, ketchup and beef stock and bring to a boil. Return the beef to the pan and heat through, about 2 minutes, before serving.

NOTE
Stir-fry beef, sliced and ready to use, is available in packages at the meat counter in most supermarkets.

ABOUT BROCCOLI

Broccoli is a member of the cabbage family and its name comes from the Italian word *brocco*, which means "branch," an apt description for this tree-like vegetable with its thick stem and tightly packed green flower heads. When buying, choose bunches that have firm, crack-free stems and tight flower heads with a deep green color. Store broccoli in a plastic bag in your refrigerator crisper for 3–4 days. Wash the broccoli well before using; there are lots of places for dirt to get trapped. Broccoli is an excellent source of vitamins A and C, iron, riboflavin and calcium.

TIPS FOR WOK COOKING

Foods prepared in a wok generally cook quickly, so cut them into uniform, bite-sized pieces to ensure they cook evenly in a minimal amount of time. Do all the chopping, slicing and measuring before you start cooking. This way you'll be ready to roll when the wok is hot and ready. Preheat the wok for a minute or two to ensure its entire cooking surface is hot. Good-quality vegetable or peanut oil is best; it doesn't burn at the high temperatures of wok cooking. After adding the oil, very carefully—you don't want it spilling out—swirl the oil around the wok to coat as much of the cooking surface as you can. Be sure to continually move the ingredients around to ensure even contact with the hottest parts of the wok. And don't add too much food at one time; the ingredients will get too little cooking time near the hot surfaces of the wok and take forever to cook, steaming rather than searing.

BANGERS with AGED CHEDDAR MASHED POTATOES

preparation time · 15 minutes
cooking time · 20–25 minutes
makes · 4 servings

The classic English "bangers and mash" is given a twist when tangy cheddar cheese is added to the mashed potatoes. Add color to this meal by serving it with steamed green beans, peas or asparagus and sliced, ripe fresh tomatoes.

ERIC'S OPTIONS

If you like, serve this with onion gravy. Fry 1 medium onion, diced, in 3 Tbsp (45 mL) of vegetable oil until tender. Mix in 3 Tbsp (45 mL) of flour and cook until the flour turns light brown. Slowly whisk in 2–2½ cups (500–625 mL) of beef stock. Simmer until thickened and season to taste with salt and pepper.

8	2–3 oz (50–75 g) beef or pork sausages	8
2 lb	russet or baking potatoes, peeled and quartered	1 kg
3 Tbsp	melted butter	45 mL
½ cup	milk	125 mL
1 cup	grated aged cheddar cheese	250 mL
2	green onions, chopped	2
to taste	salt and white pepper	to taste

Preheat the oven to 375°F (190°C). Line a roasting pan with parchment paper. Roast the sausages, turning them once, until golden and cooked through, about 20–25 minutes.

Meanwhile, boil the potatoes in lightly salted water until tender. Drain well. Thoroughly mash the potatoes and then whip in the butter and milk. Mix in the cheese, green onions, salt and pepper. Mound the potatoes on 4 plates, top with the sausages and serve immediately.

MEDITERRANEAN-STYLE BARBECUED FISH

preparation time	15 minutes	
cooking time	10–12 minutes	
makes	2 servings	

Artichokes, olives and roasted peppers give this quickly barbecued fish a Mediterranean flair. New potatoes boiled and tossed with extra virgin olive oil and chopped fresh mint or basil would nicely complement the fish.

ERIC'S OPTIONS
Replace the roasted red pepper with a fresh red bell pepper, seeded and cubed. If you like capers, sprinkle 1 Tbsp (15 mL) over the fish just before folding and sealing up the foil. If you don't have a barbecue, cook the fish in the oven at 400°F (200°C) for about 20 minutes.

2 Tbsp	extra virgin olive oil	30 mL
2	6 oz (175 g) fish fillets, such as salmon, halibut or haddock	2
2	canned artichoke hearts, drained and quartered	2
8	black olives	8
1	roasted red bell pepper, cubed (see Roasted Red Peppers, page 180)	1
to taste	salt and freshly ground black pepper	to taste
2 Tbsp	lemon juice	30 mL
1 Tbsp	homemade or store-bought pesto (see About Pesto, page 31)	15 mL

Preheat your barbecue to medium-high. Arrange 2 sheets of foil, approximately 18 × 12 inches (45 × 30 cm), one on top of the other. Brush the top with 1 Tbsp (15 mL) of the oil.

Arrange the fish in the center of the foil and scatter the artichokes, olives and bell pepper overtop; season with salt and pepper. Combine the remaining 1 Tbsp (15 mL) oil, lemon juice and pesto in a small bowl; spoon over the fish. Pull up the corners of the foil to form a packet and fold at the top to seal.

Set the foil packet on one side of the barbecue. Turn the heat underneath it to medium-low; leave the other side set to medium-high. Cook the fish for 10–12 minutes, or until just cooked through.

CHOOSING AND STORING LEMONS AND LIMES

Pick lemons and limes that are vibrantly colored, feel heavy for their size and are firm, but still have some give when squeezed. If they're extremely hard, it's a sign they're old and won't be juicy. Store lemons and limes for up to 1 week at cool room temperature and up to 3 weeks in a plastic bag in the refrigerator, depending on how fresh they were when you bought them. To extract the maximum amount of juice from lemons and limes, bring them to room temperature and roll them under the palm of your hand on a flat surface before squeezing. This will break down the membranes inside the fruit, allowing the juice to flow more freely.

KEBABS
in a PITA

preparation time	15 minutes
cooking time	6–8 minutes (depending on the type of kebab)
makes	4 servings

Most supermarkets sell meat and seafood kebabs ready to cook. They can make a fine dinner, especially when wrapped up in a pita with other tasty ingredients.

ERIC'S OPTIONS
Double the recipe and serve 2 stuffed pitas per person if the people you're feeding have large appetites.

4	4 oz (125 g) chicken, beef, lamb, pork or seafood kebabs	4
⅓ cup	tzatziki sauce (see Note)	75 mL
4	Greek-style (no pocket) pitas, warmed	4
2	ripe medium tomatoes, cubed	2
¼	long English cucumber, halved and thinly sliced	¼
1	medium yellow bell pepper, halved and sliced	1
2 cups	shredded head or leaf lettuce	500 mL

Preheat an indoor or outdoor grill to medium-high and lightly oil the bars with vegetable oil. Cook the kebabs for 3–4 minutes per side, or until completely cooked to the desired doneness (such as medium-rare for beef kebabs). Spoon 1 Tbsp (15 mL) or so of the tzatziki sauce on one side of each pita. Carefully remove the meat or seafood from the skewers and set in a row on top of the tzatziki sauce. Place the remaining ingredients in a row alongside the meat or seafood, dividing it evenly between each pita. Fold the pitas in half and serve.

NOTE
Tzatziki sauce is available in the dairy or deli section of most supermarkets.

GNOCCHI in SAGE and GARLIC BUTTER

preparation time	5 minutes
cooking time	5–6 minutes
makes	3–4 servings

Gnocchi is a plump, soft-textured, dumpling-like pasta made with potato or semolina flour. It is sold at most supermarkets and delis. It cooks quickly, so it won't be long before you're digging into this invitingly aromatic dish scented with fresh sage and garlic. Gnocchi is a filling and sustaining pasta, so to balance that richness I like to serve this dish with a simple side salad, such as baby spinach and cherry tomatoes drizzled lightly with olive oil and balsamic vinegar.

ERIC'S OPTIONS
For an even richer-tasting dish, substitute 4 oz (125 g) of crumbled Gorgonzola cheese for the Parmesan. The tangy, intense-tasting blue cheese will melt and deliciously coat the hot pasta.

2 Tbsp	butter	30 mL
1 Tbsp	extra virgin olive oil	15 mL
1	1 lb (500 g) package gnocchi	1
1–2	garlic cloves, finely chopped	1–2
12	fresh whole sage leaves	12
¼ cup	freshly grated Parmesan cheese, plus some for the table	60 mL
to taste	salt and freshly ground black pepper	to taste

Bring a large pot of lightly salted water to a boil. Set a skillet over medium heat. When the skillet is hot, add the butter and oil. When the butter starts to melt, add the gnocchi to the boiling water. When the butter has completely melted, add the garlic to the skillet and cook for 1 minute. Add the sage leaves and cook until they become very fragrant and slightly crisp on the outer edges, about 2 minutes.

When the gnocchi is tender (it will float to the top when cooked), scoop it out of the water and into the skillet. Sprinkle in the cheese, salt and pepper and toss to coat. Divide the gnocchi among pasta bowls. Serve with additional Parmesan cheese grated overtop.

FALAFEL
BURGERS

preparation time	15 minutes
cooking time	4–6 minutes
makes	4 servings

I used inexpensive falafel mix, available at most supermarkets, as the base for these vegetarian burgers that even meat-lovers will enjoy. Falafel is a Middle Eastern creation made from seasoned, ground chickpeas that are shaped into balls, fried and usually stuffed inside pita bread. Instead, I shaped the falafel mix into patties and served them in burger buns with tasty toppings.

ERIC'S OPTIONS
Instead of burger buns, stuff the patties into halved pita pockets.

1	9 oz (225 g) box falafel mix	1
3 Tbsp	vegetable oil	45 mL
4	large burger buns	4
⅓ cup	tzatziki sauce (see Note on page 143)	75 mL
4	lettuce leaves	4
to taste	tomato, cucumber, onion and feta cheese slices to taste	to taste

Place the falafel mix in a bowl. Add 1 cup (250 mL) of cold water and stir to combine. Let the mixture stand for 10 minutes. Place a large nonstick skillet over medium heat and add the oil. Moisten your hands with cold water, divide the falafel mix into 4 portions and shape each portion into a ¾-inch-thick (2 cm) patty. Fry the patties for 2–3 minutes per side, or until nicely colored and heated through. Drain on paper towels.

Spread tzatziki sauce on the buns; place a lettuce leaf on the bottom of each bun and add a patty. Top with slices of tomato, cucumber, onion and feta cheese, if desired.

STEWS, BRAISES AND ROASTS

CHICKPEA and VEGETABLE STEW

preparation time	20 minutes
cooking time	about 25 minutes
makes	4 servings

Once your fresh vegetables are chopped and sautéed, this nourishing stew will cook up in less than half an hour. Serve it over couscous, steamed rice or Mediterranean-Style Rice (page 179), and have warm wedges of pita bread alongside for dunking.

ERIC'S OPTIONS
To make this a curried stew, add 1 Tbsp (15 mL) of mild, medium or hot curry powder when mixing in the flour, and replace 1¾ cups (425 mL) of the stock with a 14 oz (398 mL) can of coconut milk.

2 Tbsp	olive oil	30 mL
2	garlic cloves, chopped	2
1	medium onion, halved and sliced	1
20	mini-carrots (see About Mini-Carrots, page 149)	20
1 tsp	paprika	5 mL
1 tsp	ground cumin	5 mL
¼ tsp	crushed chili flakes	1 mL
1 tsp	dried oregano	5 mL
2 Tbsp	all-purpose flour	30 mL
2½ cups	chicken or vegetable stock	625 mL
2	medium white-skinned potatoes, cubed	2
1	19 oz (540 mL) can chickpeas, drained well	1
½ cup	frozen peas	125 mL
to taste	salt and freshly ground black pepper	to taste

Heat the oil in a pot over medium heat. Add the garlic, onion and carrots and cook for 3–4 minutes. Mix in the paprika, cumin, chili flakes, oregano and flour and cook for 2 minutes more. Stirring constantly, slowly pour in the stock. Add the potatoes and chickpeas and bring to a gentle simmer. Cook for 15 minutes, or until the potatoes are tender. Mix in the peas and heat them through, about 2 minutes. Season with salt and pepper and serve.

ABOUT MINI-CARROTS

I always keep a bag of mini-carrots—also known as baby carrots—on hand as a quick, no-peeling-required ingredient in salads, soups, stews, stir-fries or other dishes. Good-quality mini-carrots have a bright orange color and firm, smooth, blemish-free skins. Avoid those that are soft, split or dull-looking. Mini-carrots are sold in bulk or in bags. When buying bags, always check the best-before date and examine the carrots because they may have been improperly stored. At home, keep them tightly sealed in a plastic bag in your refrigerator crisper.

HEARTY SALMON STEW

preparation time   20 minutes
cooking time   about 25 minutes
makes   4 servings

This salmon stew tastes great over Garlic Mashed Yukon Gold Potatoes (page 176).

ERIC'S OPTIONS
Substitute other fish, such as halibut or cod, for the salmon. If you prefer frozen corn, or if that's what you have on hand, use it in place of the frozen peas.

2 Tbsp	vegetable oil	30 mL
½	medium onion, thinly sliced	½
20	mini-carrots (see About Mini-Carrots, page 149)	20
1	medium celery rib, halved lengthwise and sliced	1
1	garlic clove, chopped	1
3 Tbsp	all-purpose flour	45 mL
½ tsp	dried tarragon	2 mL
2½ cups	chicken or fish stock	625 mL
1 lb	salmon fillets, cubed	500 g
½ cup	frozen peas	125 mL
to taste	salt and white pepper	to taste

Heat the oil in a large skillet over medium heat. Add the onion, carrots, celery and garlic and cook for 4–5 minutes. Stir in the flour and tarragon until well combined. Stirring constantly, slowly pour in the stock. Bring to a simmer and cook until the vegetables are tender, about 10 minutes. Add the salmon and simmer for 4–5 minutes more, or until the salmon is just cooked through. Mix in the peas and season with salt and pepper. Cook for 2 minutes more to heat the peas through.

WHY EAT SALMON?

Salmon is rich in protein, low in saturated fat and an excellent source of the polyunsaturated fatty acids, also known as omega-3 fatty acids—studies have shown that omega-3s may help reduce the risk of heart disease. Salmon is also a source of vitamin A, the B-group vitamins and vitamin D.

QUICK CHICKEN STEW
for TWO

preparation time	20 minutes
cooking time	about 20 minutes
makes	2 servings

Here's a simple, but tasty dish that, unlike stews made with tougher cuts of meat, takes minutes, not hours, to cook. If time allows, whip up a batch of Baking Powder Biscuits (page 182), to serve alongside. Any leftover biscuits will taste great with butter and jam for breakfast the day.

ERIC'S OPTIONS
Make turkey stew by replacing the chicken with boneless, skinless turkey breast or thigh.

1 Tbsp	vegetable oil	15 mL
½ lb	boneless, skinless chicken breast or thigh, cut into bite-sized cubes	250 g
⅓ cup	chopped onion	75 mL
⅓ cup	chopped carrot	75 mL
⅓ cup	chopped celery	75 mL
1½ Tbsp	all-purpose flour	22.5 mL
pinch	dried sage	pinch
1½ cups	chicken stock	375 mL
¼ cup	frozen peas or corn	60 mL
to taste	salt and freshly ground black pepper	to taste

Heat the oil in a large skillet over medium-high heat. Add the chicken, onion, carrot and celery and cook, stirring frequently, for 4–5 minutes, or until the chicken is light golden brown on all sides. Stir in the flour and sage and cook for 1 minute. Slowly add the stock, stirring constantly. Bring to a boil and reduce the heat until the stew is gently simmering. Cook until the vegetables are tender and the chicken is cooked through, about 10 minutes. (Add a little more stock if the stew becomes too thick.) Add the peas or corn and cook for 2 minutes, until heated through. Season with salt and pepper and serve immediately.

OVEN-BRAISED STEAK with ROSEMARY and GARLIC

preparation time	15 minutes	
cooking time	70–80 minutes	
makes	4 servings	

While the steak tenderizes in the oven, prepare side dishes to serve with it, such as frozen peas heated in a little melted butter and Mashed Potato Cakes with Cheddar (page 177).

ERIC'S OPTIONS
If you don't have fresh rosemary, use 1 tsp (5 mL) dried. Make oven-braised veal or pork by replacing the round steak with four 5–6 oz (150–175 g) pork or veal cutlets. Cooking method remains the same.

1½ lb	round steak, cut into 8 pieces	750 g
to taste	salt and freshly ground black pepper	to taste
1½ cups	beef stock	375 mL
2 Tbsp	all-purpose flour	30 mL
2 Tbsp	olive oil	30 mL
2	garlic cloves, chopped	2
1 Tbsp	chopped fresh rosemary	15 mL
1 Tbsp	Worcestershire sauce	15 mL

Preheat the oven to 350°F (180°C). Season the steaks with salt and pepper. Whisk the stock and flour in a bowl until smooth. Heat the oil in a skillet over medium-high heat. Add the steak and brown on both sides; transfer to a 9- x 13-inch (3.5 L) casserole.

Drain the oil from the skillet. Add the stock mixture, garlic, rosemary and Worcestershire sauce and bring to a boil. Pour the mixture over the steaks. Cover and bake until quite tender, about 65–75 minutes.

ROASTED TURKEY BREAST
with SAGE and PAN GRAVY

preparation time	15 minutes	
cooking time	75 minutes	
makes	6 servings	

Serve the turkey with mashed or steamed potatoes and Cider-Glazed Brussels Sprouts (page 172). Any leftover turkey makes great sandwiches the next day.

ERIC'S OPTIONS
To make mushroom gravy, melt 1 Tbsp (15 mL) of butter in a skillet over medium heat. Add ½ lb (250 g) of sliced white or brown mushrooms and cook until tender, about 5 minutes. Mix the mushrooms into the gravy just before serving.

2½ lb	boneless turkey breast roast (see Note, page 154)	1.25 kg
2 Tbsp	melted butter	30 mL
2 tsp	dried crumbled sage	10 mL
1 tsp	coarsely ground black pepper	5 mL
to taste	salt	to taste
2½ cups	chicken stock	625 mL
3 Tbsp	all-purpose flour	45 mL

Preheat the oven to 350°F (180°C). Place the turkey in a roasting pan. Brush with the melted butter and sprinkle with the sage, pepper and salt. Roast the turkey for 75 minutes, or until the center of the roast reaches 170°F (77°C) on an instant-read meat thermometer. Remove the turkey from the pan and set on a plate; loosely cover with foil and let it rest for 10 minutes before serving.

Meanwhile, drain the excess fat from the roasting pan and set the pan on the stovetop over medium-high heat. Whisk the stock and flour in a bowl until smooth. Add to the roasting pan and bring to a simmer, scraping the brown bits off the bottom of the pan to add taste and color to the gravy. Simmer until slightly thickened, about 4–5 minutes. Season with salt and pepper and transfer the gravy to a serving dish. Slice the turkey and serve the gravy alongside.

NOTE

Boneless turkey breast roasts, tied by the butcher to hold their shape during cooking, are available fresh at most supermarkets and butcher shops. They can be stored for 2–3 days in the refrigerator or can be frozen. If you freeze a roast, thaw it overnight in the refrigerator before roasting.

HANDLING LEFTOVERS

I'm always happy to have leftovers, whether it's soup, roasted meat, stew or any other item. Whether simply reheated or used as ingredients in another dish, they can save you time. But leftovers can cause health problems if they're improperly handled. Left at room temperature for too long, unhealthy bacteria can make the food unsafe to eat. Make sure you put leftovers into the refrigerator the moment they've cooled to room temperature, which usually takes an hour or less. To lessen the time needed to cool food such as a casserole, package it in smaller containers appropriate for reheating. To quickly cool containers of leftover foods, such as soup or chili, carefully set the container (don't submerge it!) in a sink filled with ice-cold water. Some health authorities say most leftover foods, if safely handled, will remain safe to eat for 3–4 days, but I prefer to consume them within 2 days just to be safe. If you're not sure if a leftover food is safe to eat, remember this golden rule: if in doubt, throw it out.

ROAST PORK with MCINTOSH APPLE SAUCE

preparation time	25 minutes
cooking time	60–70 minutes
makes	6 servings

A large leg roast might take over 2 hours to cook, but this lean, boneless pork loin roast cooks in an hour or a little more. You can come home from work, quickly get the roast in the oven and by the time you relax a bit and whip up a few vegetables to serve alongside, the meat is done. Any leftovers make delicious sandwiches for lunch the next day and could also be used to make Five-Minute Fried Rice (page 38).

ERIC'S OPTIONS
If time is tight, buy a jar of unsweetened applesauce instead of making your own.

2½ lb	boneless pork loin roast	1.25 kg
2 Tbsp	olive oil	30 mL
1 tsp	dried sage	5 mL
½ tsp	paprika	2 mL
to taste	salt and freshly ground black pepper	to taste
1½ cups	McIntosh Apple Sauce (see page 181)	375 mL

Preheat the oven to 450°F (230°C). Place the roast in a shallow roasting pan. Combine the oil, sage and paprika in a small bowl and brush over the pork. Sprinkle with salt and pepper. Roast for 20 minutes, and then reduce the heat to 325°F (160°C). Roast for 40–50 minutes more, or until the internal temperature reaches 160°F (71°C) on an instant-read meat thermometer inserted into the center of the roast. Remove from the oven, cover loosely with foil and allow to rest for 10 minutes. Cut into thin slices and serve the applesauce alongside.

ROAST PORK with FIVE-SPICE, HOISIN and SESAME SEEDS

preparation time	10 minutes
cooking time	45–50 minutes
makes	4 servings

This pork roast is aromatically flavored with a simple combination of five-spice powder (see About Five-Spice Powder, below) and hoisin sauce. Along with the sesame seeds used to give the pork a pleasing, crunchy exterior, that brings the number of ingredients in this tasty dish to a grand total of 4. Serve it with steamed rice and stir-fried vegetables.

ERIC'S OPTIONS
If you like spicy food, mix 1–2 tsp (5–10 mL) of Asian-style chili sauce into the hoisin sauce before brushing on the pork.

1¾ lb	boneless pork loin roast	875 g
2 tsp	five-spice powder	10 mL
⅓ cup	hoisin sauce	75 mL
1 Tbsp	sesame seeds	15 mL

Preheat the oven to 350°F (180°C). Line a shallow roasting pan with parchment paper. Set the roast in the pan and rub all over with the five-spice powder. Brush the top and sides of the roast with the hoisin sauce and sprinkle with the sesame seeds. Roast for 45–50 minutes, or until the internal temperature reaches 160°F (71°C) on an instant-read meat thermometer inserted into the center of the roast. Remove from the oven, cover loosely with foil and allow the roast to rest for 10 minutes before thinly slicing.

ABOUT FIVE-SPICE POWDER

Five-spice powder is a Chinese-style seasoning blend of—you guessed it—5 spices ground together to make a delightful mix of sweet, bitter, cool and spicy tastes. It's used in a variety of dishes, from pork and duck to stir-fried vegetables. The spices include star anise, highly aromatic, star-shaped pods with a slightly bitter, licorice-like flavor; spicy, yet cooling cloves, the nail-shaped, unopened flower bud of a tropical evergreen; and Szechuan peppercorns, a mildly hot spice made from the dried berries of the prickly ash tree (they resemble black peppercorns, but are not related). Rounding out the 5 spices are cinnamon and fennel seeds—a sweet, aromatic spice with a mild, somewhat minty, licorice-like taste.

ROAST RACK
of LAMB for TWO

preparation time | 20 minutes
cooking time | 27–35 minutes
makes | 2 servings

If you're looking for an elegant midweek meal for 2, this tender lamb has an irresistible mustard and herb crust and a delicious red wine sauce. Perfect for a special dinner; use a good-quality wine to make it and enjoy the remainder with the meal! Serve it with boiled small potatoes tossed with chopped fresh mint and Roasted Asparagus with Peppers and Pine Nuts (page 175).

ERIC'S OPTIONS
Give the sauce a sweeter taste by using port instead of red wine. If you prefer a coarser texture, coat the lamb with whole-grain Dijon mustard instead of smooth Dijon. Use 1 tsp (5 mL) chopped fresh rosemary to flavor the lamb instead of herbes de Provence.

2 Tbsp	breadcrumbs	30 mL
1 tsp	herbes de Provence (see Note, page 158)	5 mL
¼ tsp	salt	1 mL
¼ tsp	freshly ground black pepper	1 mL
1	8-rib frenched lamb rack (see Note, page 158)	1
1 Tbsp	Dijon mustard	15 mL
¼ cup	red wine	60 mL
¾ cup	beef stock	175 mL
1 Tbsp	all-purpose flour	15 mL

Preheat the oven to 400°F (200°C). Combine the breadcrumbs, herbes de Provence, salt and pepper on a plate. Cut the lamb into two 4-rib racks. Brush the top and sides of the lamb with the mustard.

Dip the mustard-coated portions of the lamb in the breadcrumb mixture, pressing the crumbs on to help them adhere. Set the lamb in a small roasting pan. Roast for 22–25 minutes for rare; 25–28 minutes for medium-rare; and 30 minutes for medium. Transfer the lamb to a plate, cover loosely with foil and let rest for 5 minutes.

Instructions continued on the next page ...

Meanwhile, place the roasting pan on the stovetop over medium-high heat. Add the wine and cook until reduced by half. Whisk the stock and flour together until smooth in a small bowl; add to the pan. Simmer until it forms a thickened sauce, about 2 minutes. To serve, pour a pool of sauce on each dinner plate and set the lamb racks on top.

NOTE

Herbes de Provence is a French-style blend made with herbs such as basil, marjoram, rosemary, fennel seed, lavender, summer savory, sage and thyme. The type and quantity of each herb used to make it can vary greatly depending on the maker. Herbes de Provence is available at most supermarkets, in bulk or in small bottles. Frenched lamb racks, with the rib bones exposed and the outer fat cap removed, are sold at most supermarkets and butcher shops.

LARGE BATCH ROAST and FREEZE MEATBALLS

preparation time	30 minutes
cooking time	40–50 minutes
makes	about 7 dozen meatballs

If you like to add meatballs to pasta sauce, or put them in a rich gravy to spoon over mashed potatoes or egg noodles, or toss them into a sweet and sour sauce to serve with fried rice, take some time on a day off and whip up a batch of these meatballs. You'll get it done quicker than you think and you'll have meatballs at the ready to add to any number of dishes, including Meatballs in Sour Cream Gravy with Parsley Noodles (page 68).

ERIC'S OPTIONS
For a more complex, meaty taste, use 1 lb (500 g) ground beef, ½ lb (250 g) ground pork and ½ lb (250 g) ground veal.

2 lb	lean ground beef	1 kg
2	large eggs, beaten	2
1 cup	breadcrumbs	250 mL
⅓ cup	milk	75 mL
3	garlic cloves, chopped	3
1 tsp	dried thyme	5 mL
4	green onions, finely chopped	4
1 tsp	salt, or to taste	5 mL
1 tsp	freshly ground black pepper	5 mL

Preheat the oven to 400°F (200°C). Line 2 rimmed baking sheets with parchment paper. Combine all the ingredients in a bowl and mix well. Moisten your hands with cold water. Roll the meat mixture into 1½-inch (4 cm) balls and place them on the baking sheets. Bake the meatballs, 1 sheet at a time, until cooked through, about 20–25 minutes. Drain off the fat and cool the meatballs to room temperature. Freeze until solid on the baking tray. Transfer to freezer bags or containers and keep frozen until needed.

ROAST SIRLOIN
au JUS

preparation time	5 minutes
cooking time	45 minutes
makes	4 servings

Quick and simple to make, this small beef roast is tender, juicy and flavorful. For a French bistro kind of meal, serve the roast with frites (a.k.a. French fries) and sautéed slices of zucchini flavored with garlic and thyme.

ERIC'S OPTIONS
Use any other small, tender beef roasts, such as strip loin, rib-eye or eye of round.

1¾ lb	top sirloin roast		875 g
2 tsp	Dijon mustard		10 mL
½ tsp	dried thyme		2 mL
to taste	salt and coarsely ground black pepper		to taste
2 cups	beef stock		500 mL

Preheat the oven to 475°F (240°C). Place the roast in a small roasting pan. Brush with the mustard and sprinkle with the thyme, salt and pepper. Roast for 10 minutes, then reduce the heat to 325°F (160°C) and roast for 30 minutes more. (This should yield a rare to medium-rare roast. Cook for 10–15 minutes longer if you like your beef medium to medium-well done.) Transfer the roast to a plate, cover loosely with foil and allow to rest for 10 minutes before thinly slicing.

Meanwhile, set the roasting pan on the stovetop over medium-high heat. Add the stock and bring to a simmer, scraping the bottom of the pan to release the tasty brown bits on the bottom. Pour the jus into a gravy boat and serve alongside the beef for drizzling on top.

ROAST BEEF on a BUN
with BARBECUE DIPPING SAUCE

preparation time	15 minutes
cooking time	45 minutes
makes	4 servings

Make this a diner-style supper by serving it with pickles, corn on the cob and Quick Coleslaw with Apples, Raisins and Pecans (page 166).

ERIC'S OPTIONS			
To add a smoky, spicy taste to the dipping sauce, add a finely chopped canned chipotle pepper to the pan before you bring the sauce to a simmer.	1¾ lb	top round or sirloin roast	875 g
	1 Tbsp	olive oil	15 mL
	2 tsp	Cajun spice or seasoning salt	10 mL
	1 cup	beef stock	250 mL
	1 cup	barbecue sauce	250 mL
	½ cup	water	125 mL
	4	kaiser buns	4

Preheat the oven to 475°F (240°C). Place the meat in a small roasting pan. Brush with the olive oil and rub with the Cajun spice or seasoning salt. Roast for 10 minutes, then reduce the heat to 325°F (160°C) and roast for 30 minutes more. (This should yield a rare to medium-rare roast. Cook for 10–15 minutes longer if you like your beef cooked medium to medium-well done.) Transfer the roast to a plate, cover loosely with foil and allow to rest for 10 minutes.

While the roast rests, drain the fat from the pan and set on the stovetop over medium-high heat. Add the stock, barbecue sauce and water and bring to a boil, scraping the pan to release the tasty brown bits on the bottom. Reduce the heat until the sauce gently simmers and cook for 3–4 minutes. Thinly slice the beef and pile it on the buns. Serve a bowl of sauce alongside each bun for dipping.

SPLENDID SIDES

CHAPTER NINE

FAMILY-STYLE SALAD with BACON RANCH DRESSING

preparation time · 20 minutes
cooking time · 5 minutes
makes · 4–6 servings

Crisp lettuce, colorful vegetables and a tangy dressing combine in a salad the whole family will enjoy. The dressing can be made a day or two in advance and kept refrigerated until needed.

ERIC'S OPTIONS
Substitute 6–8 cups (1.5–2 L) of organic mixed salad greens or baby spinach for the lettuce. Top the salad with any raw vegetable that appeals, such as sliced cucumber, radish, mushroom or red onion. Substitute a store-bought ranch dressing if there's no time to make your own.

FOR THE DRESSING:

¼ cup	light mayonnaise	60 mL
¼ cup	buttermilk	60 mL
½ tsp	sugar	2 mL
1 Tbsp	lemon juice	15 mL
1	green onion, finely chopped	1
4	slices side bacon, cooked until crisp and finely crumbled	4
to taste	salt and freshly ground black pepper	to taste

Combine all the ingredients and thoroughly mix. Store in the refrigerator until needed.

FOR THE SALAD:

1	head leaf or iceberg lettuce, chopped	1
1	medium yellow bell pepper, cut into strips	1
12–15	cherry tomatoes, halved	12–15
1½ cups	small broccoli florets	375 mL
1½ cups	small cauliflower florets	375 mL
1	medium carrot, thinly sliced	1

Mound the chopped lettuce on a platter. Arrange the rest of the vegetables artfully overtop. Serve with the dressing alongside for drizzling on top.

QUICK COLESLAW with APPLES, RAISINS and PECANS

preparation time · 10 minutes
cooking time · none
makes · 6 servings

Coleslaw mix, usually consisting of shredded red and green cabbage and carrots, is available at every supermarket. That convenient product enables you to quickly whip up this coleslaw, which is dressed up with a sweet and sour dressing, apples, raisins and pecans. This salad goes particularly well with the Slow Cooker Pork Back Ribs in Barbecue Sauce (page 92).

ERIC'S OPTIONS
If you like curry, whisk 1–2 tsp (5–10 mL) of curry powder into the oil and vinegar mixture before tossing in the other ingredients. To make your own coleslaw mix, combine 3½ cups (875 mL) of shredded green and/or red cabbage with 1 grated medium carrot.

2 Tbsp	vegetable oil	30 mL
¼ cup	apple cider vinegar	60 mL
2 Tbsp	granulated sugar	30 mL
to taste	salt and freshly ground black pepper	to taste
4 cups	coleslaw mix	1 L
1	medium apple, cut into small cubes	1
⅓ cup	raisins	75 mL
⅓ cup	pecan pieces	75 mL
3	green onions, finely chopped	3

Place the oil, vinegar, sugar, salt and pepper in a large salad bowl and whisk to combine. Add the remaining ingredients, toss to combine and serve.

WARM POTATO SALAD
with SNAP PEAS and MINT

preparation time	·	15 minutes
cooking time	·	12–15 minutes
makes	·	4 servings

Here's a lighter—that is, no mounds of mayonnaise—version of potato salad accented with bright green snap peas and refreshing mint. It's served warm so you can enjoy it the moment it's tossed together, no chilling required. For a quick supper, serve it with a simply cooked main course, such as grilled lamb chops or baked salmon fillets.

ERIC'S OPTIONS
If snap peas are unavailable, use snow peas. Or replace the peas with ½ lb (250 g) fresh asparagus; trim and discard the lower stalks, slice the spears into 2-inch (5 cm) pieces and cook as you would the snap peas.

16	small new white or red potatoes, halved	16
3 Tbsp	extra virgin olive oil	45 mL
1 Tbsp	freshly squeezed lemon juice	15 mL
pinch	granulated sugar	pinch
1	garlic clove, crushed	1
24	snap peas, trimmed	24
to taste	salt and freshly ground black pepper	to taste
3 Tbsp	chopped fresh mint	45 mL
½	small red onion, halved and thinly sliced	½

Place the potatoes in a pot, cover with a generous amount of lightly salted cold water and bring to a boil. Boil until just tender, about 10 minutes.

Meanwhile, place the oil, lemon juice, sugar and garlic in a salad bowl and whisk to combine.

When the potatoes are barely tender, add the snap peas and cook until crisp-tender, about 2 minutes. Drain the vegetables well and transfer to the salad bowl. Add the salt, pepper, mint and red onion. Toss to combine and serve.

GRILLED CORN
with LIME and CUMIN

preparation time · 10 minutes
cooking time · 4–5 minutes
makes · 4 servings

Serve this corn with just about anything cooked on the barbecue, such as steaks, chicken, salmon, ribs and burgers. Cooking the shucked corn directly over the heat slightly chars and caramelizes the kernels—very tasty!

ERIC'S OPTIONS
For spicy grilled corn, add ¼ tsp (1 mL) of cayenne pepper to the butter mixture.

2 Tbsp	butter	30 mL
1 tsp	ground cumin	5 mL
2 Tbsp	freshly squeezed lime juice	30 mL
4	cobs of corn, shucked	4
to taste	salt and freshly ground black pepper	to taste
4	lime wedges	4

Preheat your barbecue or indoor grill to medium. Place the butter, cumin and lime juice in a small skillet over medium heat and cook just until the butter melts. Stir to combine and then remove from the heat. Place the corn on the grill. Cook, turning from time to time, until the corn is lightly charred and just tender, about 4–5 minutes. Set the corn on a platter. Brush with the butter mixture, sprinkle with salt and pepper and serve immediately, garnished with lime wedges.

GREEN BEAN STIR-FRY

preparation time · 5 minutes
cooking time · 5 minutes
makes · 4 servings

This colorful vegetable side dish goes great with salmon, chicken and pork. It can also make a light supper when served over steamed rice.

ERIC'S OPTIONS
For an even more colorful dish, use a mix of wax and green beans. If you like things spicy, add 1 tsp (5 mL) of Asian-style chili sauce with the teriyaki sauce. Replace the beans with ¾ lb (375 g) fresh asparagus; trim and discard the lower stalks, slice the spears into 2-inch (5 cm) pieces and cook as you would the green beans.

1 Tbsp	vegetable oil	15 mL
½ lb	green beans, trimmed	250 g
1	8 oz (228 mL) can sliced water chestnuts, drained well	1
1	medium red bell pepper, cubed	1
3 Tbsp	teriyaki sauce	45 mL
2 Tbsp	orange juice	30 mL

Heat the oil in a large skillet over medium-high heat. Add the beans, water chestnuts and bell pepper and stir-fry for 2 minutes. Add the teriyaki sauce and orange juice and cook until it forms a slightly thickened sauce, about 2 minutes. Serve immediately.

ABOUT WATER CHESTNUTS

Despite their name, water chestnuts are not a nut—they are the edible tuber of an aquatic plant native to Southeast Asia. It's likely they got the name from their shape and rich brown skin, which looks somewhat like the nut. You can tell the two are not related once you peel away the skin. The white flesh of a water chestnut is crisp and potato-like in texture, mild and slightly sweet-tasting. Its main appeal is the crunchiness it adds to salads, soups, stuffing and stir-fries. Water chestnuts are sold, fully cooked, sliced or whole, in cans. To freshen up the taste of canned water chestnuts, I rinse them with cold water and drain them well before using. You can sometimes find fresh water chestnuts for sale, particularly in Asian markets. After peeling them, keep them immersed in water until needed to prevent them from oxidizing. Raw water chestnuts will need a few minutes of cooking to make them crisp-tender, so factor that in when deciding when to add them to dishes such as a stir-fry. Water chestnuts are low in calories, are a good source of vitamin B and fiber and contain calcium and iron.

CIDER-GLAZED
BRUSSELS SPROUTS

preparation time ·	5 minutes
cooking time	6–8 minutes
makes ·	4 servings

Sweet apple cider helps tame the intense flavor of Brussels sprouts. This side dish goes particularly well with poultry and pork, such as Roasted Turkey Breast with Sage and Pan Gravy (page 153) or Crispy Oven-Baked Pork Cutlets (page 114).

ERIC'S OPTIONS
For a richer taste, toss in ⅓ cup (75 mL) of lightly toasted walnut or pecan pieces just before serving.

1 lb	small to medium Brussels sprouts, trimmed	500 g
½ cup	apple cider (nonalcoholic)	125 mL
1 Tbsp	butter	15 mL
to taste	salt and freshly ground black pepper	to taste

Bring a large pot of water to a boil. Add the Brussels sprouts, return to a boil and boil for 3–4 minutes, or until crisp-tender. Drain well, cool in ice-cold water, and drain well again. Place the apple cider and butter in a large skillet and bring to a boil over high heat. Add the Brussels sprouts, lower the heat to medium and simmer until the Brussels sprouts are tender and the cider mixture is a little syrupy, about 3–4 minutes. Season with salt and pepper and serve immediately.

MINI-CARROTS with HONEY, GINGER and LEMON

preparation time · 5 minutes
cooking time · 7–8 minutes
makes · 4 servings

Peeled and ready to use, mini-carrots take just minutes to cook. In this recipe, the flavor goes up several notches thanks to the addition of sweet honey, spicy fresh ginger and tart lemon juice. I like to dress up simply cooked main dishes, such as grilled or sautéed boneless, skinless chicken breasts or baked ham, with this tasty dish.

ERIC'S OPTIONS
For a different sweet taste, use maple syrup instead of honey. Instead of mini-carrots, peel an equal weight of regular carrots and slice into coins.

1 lb	mini-carrots (see About Mini-Carrots, page 149)	500 g
2 Tbsp	butter	30 mL
1 tsp	freshly grated ginger, or to taste	5 mL
1 Tbsp	honey	15 mL
1 Tbsp	freshly squeezed lemon juice	15 mL
to taste	salt and freshly ground black pepper	to taste
1 Tbsp	chopped fresh parsley (optional)	15 mL

Place the carrots in a pot, cover with cold water and set over medium-high heat. Bring to a boil and cook until just tender. Drain and return the pot to the stove over low heat. Add the butter, ginger, honey, lemon juice, salt and pepper to the carrots and cook, stirring, until the butter melts and the carrots are nicely coated, about 2 minutes. Sprinkle in the parsley, if using, and serve.

Roasted Asparagus with Peppers and Pine Nuts (facing page)
and Mini-Carrots with Honey, Ginger and Lemon (page 173)

ROASTED ASPARAGUS
with PEPPERS and PINE NUTS

preparation time · 10 minutes
cooking time · 21 minutes
makes · 4 servings

Red peppers and pine nuts add richness and color to this simple but divine asparagus dish.

ERIC'S OPTIONS
This dish also tastes fine at room temperature, so don't worry if it cools down before you serve it.

1 lb	asparagus, stems trimmed	500 g
3 Tbsp	olive oil	45 mL
1 Tbsp	balsamic vinegar	15 mL
¼ cup	finely chopped red bell pepper	60 mL
2 Tbsp	pine nuts	30 mL
to taste	salt and freshly ground black pepper	to taste

Preheat the oven to 400°F (200°C). Bring a pot of water to a boil, add the asparagus and cook for 1 minute. Drain well, immerse in ice-cold water and drain well again.

Place the asparagus in a single layer in a baking dish. Drizzle with the olive oil and balsamic vinegar; sprinkle with the red pepper, pine nuts, salt and pepper. Roast for 20 minutes and serve.

BUYING, STORING AND PREPARING ASPARAGUS

Fresh asparagus will have tightly closed tips and smooth, straight, firm stems. The cut end of the asparagus should not be dry or gray in color; if it is, the asparagus is either old or was improperly stored. For the best flavor, cook asparagus the day you buy it. If you have to store it, seal it in a plastic bag and place in the refrigerator crisper for up to 3 or 4 days. Asparagus is often grown in sandy soil, so wash it well before you cook it. To prepare it, hold the tip firmly in one hand and use your other hand to bend the spear; the lower, woody part will snap off at its natural breaking point. You can keep the lower part of stem, if it's not too tough, to use in soup.

GARLIC MASHED YUKON GOLD POTATOES

preparation time · 5 minutes
cooking time · about 15 minutes
makes · 4–6 servings

No peeling in this recipe: the skin of Yukon Gold potatoes adds a pleasing, almost nutty taste to the dish.

ERIC'S OPTIONS
For really rich-tasting potatoes, mix ½ cup (125 mL) of crumbled blue cheese into the potatoes before you season them with salt and pepper. For added color, mix in 2–3 finely chopped greens onions.

2 lb	Yukon Gold potatoes, washed well and quartered	1 kg
4–6	garlic cloves, thickly sliced	4–6
⅓–½ cup	milk	75–125 mL
2 Tbsp	butter	30 mL
to taste	salt and white pepper	to taste

Gently boil the potatoes and garlic in a generous amount of lightly salted water until both are very tender. Drain well and thoroughly mash. Whip in the milk and butter until well combined and the potatoes are lightened. Season with salt and white pepper and serve immediately.

MASHED POTATO CAKES
with CHEDDAR

preparation time · 20 minutes
cooking time · 6–8 minutes
makes · 4 servings

In the winter, I often serve a side dish of mashed potatoes at Sunday dinner, and I always make extra. During the week, I can make these comforting potato cakes with the leftovers.

ERIC'S OPTIONS
You can form and bread the cakes several hours ahead of time. Cover and refrigerate until you're ready to fry them.

2 cups	leftover mashed potatoes	500 mL
½ cup	grated cheddar cheese	125 mL
1	large egg, beaten	1
2	green onions, finely chopped	2
to taste	salt and white pepper	to taste
pinch	ground nutmeg	pinch
⅓ cup	breadcrumbs	75 mL
3 Tbsp	vegetable oil	45 mL

Combine the potatoes, cheese, egg, green onion, salt, white pepper and nutmeg in a medium bowl and mix well. Spread the breadcrumbs on a large plate. Moisten your hands with cold water and shape ¼-cup (60 mL) measures of the potato mixture into 1-inch-thick (2.5 cm) cakes. Coat both sides of the cakes with breadcrumbs, gently pressing the crumbs on to help them adhere.

Heat the oil in a large nonstick skillet over medium heat. Cook the cakes for 3–4 minutes per side, or until golden brown and heated through.

ROASTED POTATO WEDGES
with CHILI and PARMESAN

preparation time · 10 minutes
cooking time · 40 minutes
makes · 4 servings

These full-flavored spuds are great with barbecued steaks, ribs, chicken and fish.

ERIC'S OPTIONS
Use 3–4 large Yukon Gold potatoes instead of baking potatoes. If you like cilantro, substitute 2 Tbsp (30 mL), chopped, for the green onions. The pungent taste of cilantro complements the chili powder, cumin and hot pepper sauce in this dish.

3	large baking potatoes, washed well and patted dry	3
2–3 Tbsp	olive oil	30–45 mL
1 Tbsp	chili powder	15 mL
½ tsp	ground cumin	2 mL
1 tsp	hot pepper sauce, such as Tabasco	5 mL
to taste	salt	to taste
⅓ cup	freshly grated Parmesan cheese	75 mL
2	green onions, chopped	2

Preheat the oven to 375°F (190°C). Line a baking sheet with parchment paper. Cut the potatoes in half lengthwise; cut each half into 4–6 long wedges. Place in a large bowl and add the oil, chili powder, cumin, hot sauce and salt. Toss to coat all the surfaces of the potatoes.

Place the potatoes in a single layer on the baking sheet and roast for 40 minutes, turning once halfway through the cooking to ensure even browning. Arrange the potatoes on a large serving platter; sprinkle with the Parmesan and green onions and serve.

MEDITERRANEAN-STYLE RICE

preparation time	·	15 minutes
cooking time	·	about 20 minutes
makes	·	4 servings

Roasted peppers, garlic and fresh basil give this rice a Mediterranean-style taste. Serve it with stews, kebabs, roasted or grilled chicken or pork, or baked fish.

ERIC'S OPTIONS
If you don't eat meat, use vegetable stock instead of chicken stock.

2 Tbsp	olive oil	30 mL
½	medium onion, finely chopped	½
1 cup	long-grain white rice	250 mL
2	garlic cloves, chopped	2
1	roasted red pepper, finely chopped (see Roasted Red Peppers, page 180)	1
1 tsp	ground cumin	5 mL
¼ tsp	paprika	1 mL
dash	cayenne pepper	dash
1½ cups	chicken stock	375 mL
to taste	salt and freshly ground black pepper	to taste
¼ cup	chopped fresh basil	60 mL

Heat the oil in a medium-sized pot over medium heat. Add the onion and cook until tender, about 3–4 minutes. Stir in the rice and garlic and cook for 2–3 minutes more. Add the roasted pepper, cumin, paprika, cayenne, stock, salt and pepper; increase the heat to high. Bring to a boil, cover and reduce the heat to its lowest setting. Cook until the rice is tender, about 15 minutes. Stir the basil into the rice and serve immediately.

ROASTED RED PEPPERS

Roasted red peppers are sold in jars or in bulk at most supermarkets, usually in the deli department. If time allows, you also could roast your own peppers. Preheat the oven to 400°F (200°C). Place the peppers in a baking pan lined with parchment paper. Roast, turning once or twice, until the peppers begin to char and blister, about 30–35 minutes. Set the peppers on a plate, cover with foil and cool to room temperature. Peel the peppers; the skin should just slip off. Cut each pepper in half and remove the seeds. The peppers are now ready to cut and use as desired.

MCINTOSH
APPLE SAUCE

preparation time · 15 minutes
cooking time · about 20 minutes
makes · about 3–4 cups (750 mL–1L)

I like to use McIntosh apples to make applesauce for 3 reasons. They're sweet enough that you don't have to add much or any sugar; they have just enough acidity to balance that sweetness; and they have a wonderful aroma that makes this sauce not just taste good, but also smell good.

ERIC'S OPTIONS
If you want a completely smooth sauce, pulse the cooked apples in a food processor for a few seconds until smooth. Try other apple varieties, such as Spartan, Fuji or Jonagold, or use a mix of apples.

8	medium McIntosh apples, peeled, cored and sliced	8
½ cup	water	125 mL
1 Tbsp	lemon juice	15 mL
to taste	granulated sugar (optional)	to taste
pinch	salt and cinnamon (optional)	pinch

Place all the ingredients in a pot over medium heat. Bring to a gentle simmer and cook, stirring occasionally, until the apple slices break apart and dissolve into a sauce, about 15–20 minutes. Add additional water during cooking if required. When the sauce has achieved the desired consistency, remove from the heat. Cool to room temperature, transfer to a tightly sealed container and store in the refrigerator for up to a week. This sauce can also be frozen for up to 2 months.

BAKING POWDER
BISCUITS

preparation time · 20 minutes
cooking time · 15 minutes
makes · about 15 biscuits

Serve these biscuits with soups, stews and roast chicken. Leftover biscuits are great for breakfast the next morning: stuff them with a fried egg or top with homemade jam or marmalade.

ERIC'S OPTIONS
This recipe can be halved. Make savory herbed biscuits by mixing 2 tsp (10 mL) of finely chopped fresh rosemary, thyme or sage into the flour mixture before adding the milk.

4 cups	all-purpose flour	1 L
2 Tbsp	baking powder	30 mL
2 tsp	sugar	10 mL
2 tsp	salt	10 mL
⅔ cup	vegetable shortening	150 mL
1¼–1¾ cups	milk	310–425 mL
2 Tbsp	melted butter	30 mL

Preheat the oven to 400°F (200°C). Line a baking sheet with parchment paper. Place the flour, baking powder, sugar and salt in a large bowl and whisk to combine. Cut in the shortening, using a pastry knife, 2 forks or your fingertips, until the mixture resembles a pea-sized crumble. Using a fork, stir in 1¼ cups (310 mL) of milk, adding more as needed until the dough leaves the side of the bowl and starts to form a ball. (Too much milk will result in sticky dough, too little and the biscuits will be dry and fall apart.)

Place the dough on a lightly floured surface and lightly knead a few times, about 30 seconds. Press into a round about 1 inch (2.5 cm) thick. Use a floured 3-inch (8 cm) round cookie cutter to cut out the biscuits. Place them on the baking sheet about 2 inches (5 cm) apart. Form the remaining scraps of dough into another round and cut more biscuits. Brush the tops with melted butter. Bake for 15 minutes, or until lightly browned and puffed up.

SIMPLE SWEETS

CHAPTER TEN

ORANGE PINEAPPLE
ICE POPS

preparation time · 5 minutes
cooking time · a few minutes
makes · about 16 popsicles

Serve these icy and refreshing, juice-filled treats for dessert on a warm summer evening. You'll need a Popsicle mold or two to make these.

ERIC'S OPTIONS
You can make these ice pops with just about any combination of juice you like; try apple and cranberry, or peach and pear. Adjust the amount of sugar upwards or downwards depending on the sweetness of the juices.

1 cup	unsweetened pineapple juice	250 mL
⅓ cup	granulated sugar, or to taste	75 mL
2½ cups	unsweetened orange juice	625 mL
¼ cup	freshly squeezed lime juice	60 mL

Place the pineapple juice and sugar in a medium pot. Set over medium-high heat and stir just until the sugar is completely dissolved. Remove from the heat and stir in the orange juice and lime juice. Pour the mixture into the mold, set in the sticks and freeze until solid. Keep frozen until ready to serve.

SLICED PEACHES with ICE CREAM and STRAWBERRY SAUCE

preparation time · 10 minutes
cooking time · none
makes · 4 servings

Here's a colorful dessert featuring 2 classic and irresistible summer tastes—peach and strawberry.

ERIC'S OPTIONS
When fresh peaches are unavailable, you can use canned sliced peaches. In summer, when local strawberries are in season, make a large batch of the sauce and freeze some for later use.

1 cup	sliced strawberries	250 mL
2 Tbsp	icing sugar, or to taste	30 mL
4	scoops vanilla ice cream	4
4	ripe peaches, pitted and sliced	4
for garnish	mint sprigs (optional)	for garnish

Place the strawberries and icing sugar in a food processor and purée until smooth. Place a scoop of ice cream in each of 4 dessert bowls. Arrange the peach slices evenly on top of the ice cream. Spoon the strawberry sauce over the peaches. Garnish with mint sprigs, if desired, and enjoy.

ABOUT PEACHES

Walk up to a display of peaches at a supermarket or farm stand and if they're fresh and of good quality, you should be wonderfully overwhelmed by an intoxicating aroma that's somewhere between sparkling wine and honey. When you lift up a prime peach, the skin will feel velvety and the fruit should feel heavy for its size, a sign it will be very juicy. When squeezed gently, a ripe peach should give slightly. If you've bought peaches that aren't quite ripe, you can speed up the ripening process by placing them in a sealed paper bag. Store them at room temperature and they should be ready to eat in a day or two.

EASY-PEASY LEMON PIE

preparation time	10 minutes
cooking time	20 minutes
makes	8 servings

This pie is a snap to make, but it needs to chill in the refrigerator after baking, so make it the night before you want to serve it. Just keep a close eye on the refrigerator, as goblins in the night may want to have a slice before tomorrow's dinner bell rings.

ERIC'S OPTIONS
Make key lime pie by replacing the lemon zest and juice with an equal amount of key lime zest and juice.

2	large eggs	2
2	10 oz (300 mL) cans sweetened condensed milk	2
1 Tbsp	finely grated lemon zest	15 mL
½ cup	freshly squeezed lemon juice	125 mL
1	9-inch (23 cm) graham cracker pie crust (see Note)	1
½ cup	whipping cream	125 mL
1 Tbsp	icing sugar, or to taste	15 mL
for garnish	mint springs (optional)	for garnish

Place an oven rack in the middle position. Preheat the oven to 325°F (160°C). Crack the eggs into a bowl. Whisk in the condensed milk and the lemon zest and juice. Pour the mixture into the pie crust. Bake for 20 minutes.

Cool the pie to room temperature on a baking rack. Cover and chill in the refrigerator for at least 2 hours.

Whip the cream until soft peaks form. Whip in the icing sugar and continue beating until stiff peaks form. Cut the pie into wedges. Top each wedge with a dollop of whipped cream just before serving. Garnish with mint spring, if desired.

NOTE
Graham cracker pie crusts are available at most supermarkets.

SKILLET
S'MORES

preparation time · 2–3 minutes
cooking time · 4–6 minutes
makes · 4 servings

Here's a cook-at-home version of the sweet treat kids love to make when camping. You won't have the ambience of the campground, but the melted marshmallow and chocolate chips stuffed inside the cookies will taste just as good.

ERIC'S OPTIONS
Make chocolate caramel smores by using a mix of chocolate and caramel chips.

4	marshmallows, each cut into 3 slices	4
8	large, round digestive cookies	8
4 Tbsp	chocolate chips	60 mL

Set a large nonstick skillet over medium-low heat. Set out 4 cookies and top each with 3 slices of marshmallow and 1 Tbsp (15 mL) of chocolate chips. Cover each with another cookie. Set the stuffed cookies in the skillet and cover. Cook for 2–3 minutes; turn the cookies over and cook for 2–3 minutes more, or until the marshmallows and chocolate chips begin to melt and become gooey. Cool slightly before devouring.

BAKE and FREEZE
CARROT CAKE SQUARES

preparation time	40 minutes
cooking time	35–40 minutes
makes	18 servings

This recipe is for 2 cakes yielding a total of 18 squares that freeze very well. For a quick midweek dessert, pull the required number of squares out of the freezer and thaw at room temperature for about 30 minutes. This moist and delicious cake substitutes applesauce for the usual oil, making it a little bit lighter.

ERIC'S OPTIONS
Instead of walnut or pecan halves, top each cake square with a bit of lightly toasted, unsweetened shredded coconut. I like a thick layer of cream cheese icing on my carrot carrot. If you don't, cut the ingredients required for the icing in half and spread a thinner layer of icing on each cake.

1½ cups	granulated sugar	375 mL
1 cup	unsweetened applesauce	250 mL
4	large eggs	4
1 tsp	pure vanilla extract	5 mL
2 cups	all-purpose flour	500 mL
2 tsp	baking soda	10 mL
2 tsp	baking powder	10 mL
½ tsp	salt	2 mL
2 tsp	ground cinnamon	10 mL
¼ tsp	ground nutmeg	1 mL
3 cups	grated carrot	750 mL
1 cup	chopped walnuts or pecans	250 mL
⅔ cup	raisins	150 mL
1	½ lb (250 g) package cream cheese, at room temperature	1
½ cup	butter, at room temperature	125 mL
3 cups	icing sugar	750 mL
18	walnut or pecan halves	18

Instructions follow on page 191 ...

BAKE and FREEZE
CARROT CAKE SQUARES (CONTINUED)

Place an oven rack in the middle position. Preheat the oven to 350°F (180°C). Cut two 8- × 12-inch (20 × 30 cm) pieces of parchment paper and fit them into the bottom and up 2 sides of two 8-inch-square (2 L) baking pans. (The parchment paper extending up the sides will help lift the cake out of the pan once it's baked.)

Combine the granulated sugar, applesauce, eggs and vanilla in a large bowl and beat well. Whisk the flour, baking soda, baking powder, salt, cinnamon and nutmeg together in a separate bowl. Add the flour mixture to the applesauce mixture and stir until just combined. Stir in the carrot, chopped nuts and raisins. Spoon the batter into the prepared pans, dividing it evenly. Bake for 35–40 minutes, or until a cake tester inserted into the middle of the cake comes out clean. Cool the cake on a rack to room temperature.

Place the cream cheese and butter in a bowl and beat until thoroughly combined and lightened. Beat in the icing sugar until fully incorporated. Lift the cakes out of their pans. Spread the icing on the tops of both cakes. Chill the cake in the refrigerator until the icing is set before cutting into squares.

Cut each cake into 9 squares and top each square with half a walnut or pecan. Wrap each piece individually in wax paper or plastic wrap, place in an airtight container and freeze until needed.

MOIST and DELICIOUS ONE-PAN CHOCOLATE CAKE

preparation time · 10 minutes
cooking time · 35–40 minutes
makes · 9 servings

How easy can it get? This is a family-style cake that you mix right in the baking pan!

ERIC'S OPTIONS
For an elegant touch, serve slices of cake on a pool of strawberry sauce (see Sliced Peaches with Ice Cream and Strawberry Sauce, page 185).

1¼ cups	all-purpose flour	310 mL
1 cup	granulated sugar	250 mL
¼ cup	cornstarch	60 mL
¼ cup	unsweetened cocoa powder	60 mL
1 tsp	baking soda	5 mL
½ tsp	ground cinnamon	2 mL
½ tsp	salt	2 mL
1 cup	milk	250 mL
⅓ cup	vegetable oil	75 mL
1 Tbsp	lemon juice	15 mL
1 tsp	pure vanilla extract	5 mL
	whipped cream or ice cream (optional)	

Place an oven rack in the middle position. Preheat the oven to 350°F (180°C). Place the flour, sugar, cornstarch, cocoa, baking soda, cinnamon and salt in a nonstick 8-inch-square (2 L) baking pan. Mix with a fork or small whisk until well combined. Add the milk, oil, lemon juice and vanilla and mix until well combined. Bake for 35–40 minutes, or until a cake tester inserted in the center comes out clean. Cool on a rack for at least 15 minutes before cutting. (It can be served warm or at room temperature.) Serve plain or, if desired, top with a dollop of whipped cream or a scoop of vanilla ice cream.

HOT CARAMEL
PUDDING CAKE

preparation time	15 minutes
cooking time	25 minutes
makes	6–8 servings

Hot caramel pudding and cake all in one dish—it doesn't get better than that!

ERIC'S OPTIONS
If you're feeling very sinful, sprinkle the top of the pudding cake with ¼ cup (60 mL) of shaved milk or dark chocolate directly after you remove it from the oven. The heat from the cake will melt the chocolate by the time you're ready to serve it, giving it a heavenly caramel and chocolate flavor.

1 cup	all-purpose flour	250 mL
2 tsp	baking powder	10 mL
¼ tsp	salt	1 mL
1½ cups	lightly packed golden brown sugar	375 mL
¼ cup	raisins	60 mL
¼ cup	pecan pieces	60 mL
½ cup	milk	125 mL
2 cups	boiling water	500 mL
2 Tbsp	butter	30 mL
½ tsp	pure vanilla extract	2 mL
½ tsp	ground cinnamon	2 mL
	whipped cream, ice cream or frozen yogurt (optional)	

Place an oven rack in the middle position. Preheat the oven to 375°F (190°C). Lightly spray an 8-inch-square (2 L) baking pan with vegetable oil. Using a whisk, combine the flour, baking powder, salt and ½ cup (125 mL) of the brown sugar together in a bowl. Stir in the raisins and pecans. Mix in the milk to form a thick batter. Spoon and spread the batter into the prepared pan.

Use a whisk to combine the boiling water, remaining 1 cup (250 mL) of brown sugar, butter, vanilla and cinnamon in another bowl. Pour the mixture over the cake batter. Bake for 25 minutes.

Transfer to a rack and allow to set for 15–20 minutes. Spoon into a bowls and, if desired, top with a dollop of whipped cream or a scoop of vanilla ice cream or frozen yogurt.

SWEET and TANGY LEMON PUDDING CAKE

preparation time	15 minutes	
cooking time	45–50 minutes	
makes	6–8 servings	

Another cake with a pudding-like texture, this one is sweet and tangy. I like to get it into the oven just before sitting down to dinner so it's ready shortly after the main course is done.

ERIC'S OPTIONS
Make the presentation extra special by topping each portion with a mix of whole or sliced fresh berries, such as raspberries, blueberries, blackberries and strawberries.

2 Tbsp	butter, at room temperature, plus some for the dish	30 mL
½ cup	granulated sugar	125 mL
2	large eggs, separated	2
¼ cup	all-purpose flour	60 mL
2 cups	milk	500 mL
2 tsp	finely grated lemon zest	10 mL
¼ cup	freshly squeezed lemon juice	60 mL

Place an oven rack in the middle position. Preheat the oven to 350°F (180°C). Lightly butter an 8-inch-square (2 L) baking dish. Beat the 2 Tbsp (30 mL) butter and sugar together in a bowl until well combined. Beat in the egg yolks. Mix in the flour, then the milk, lemon zest and lemon juice (the batter will be thin). In another bowl, beat the egg whites until soft peaks form. Whisk the beaten egg whites into the batter. Spoon the batter into the baking dish. Bake for 45–50 minutes, or until the top is set and light golden. Cool on a rack for 15 minutes before serving.

APPLE BLUEBERRY CRUMBLE

preparation time	20 minutes	
cooking time	35–40 minutes	
makes	6 servings	

Comforting crumbles: easy to make at the last minute, aromatic and delicious. This one features 2 fruits that are always available—fresh or frozen in the case of blueberries—at any time of the year.

ERIC'S OPTIONS

Two other tasty combinations: replace the apples with 3 medium pears, peeled, cored and sliced; substitute 4 medium nectarines, pitted and sliced, for the apples.

FOR THE FILLING:

3	medium apples, peeled, cored and sliced into thin wedges	3
1½ cups	fresh or frozen blueberries	375 mL
¼ cup	packed golden brown sugar	60 mL
½ cup	apple juice	125 mL
1 Tbsp	lemon juice	15 mL
2 Tbsp	all-purpose flour	30 mL

Combine the filling ingredients in a bowl and spoon into an 8-inch-square (2 L) baking dish. Place an oven rack in the middle position. Preheat the oven to 350°F (180°C).

FOR THE TOPPING:

1 cup	rolled oats	250 mL
¼ cup	butter, at room temperature	60 mL
¼ cup	packed golden brown sugar	60 mL
½ tsp	cinnamon	2 mL
pinch	ground cloves	pinch
pinch	ground nutmeg	pinch
2 Tbsp	all-purpose flour	30 mL

Combine the topping ingredients in a bowl until they're well mixed and have a crumbly texture. Sprinkle over the filling.

Bake for 35–40 minutes, until golden brown and bubbling. Serve warm or at room temperature.

ABOUT BLUEBERRIES

When buying blueberries, choose firm (not hard) ones with a uniform blue color frosted with a silvery sheen. When you get them home, discard any that are soft or shriveled. Keep them in the container you bought them in, loosely covered, and store in the refrigerator for 4–5 days. Don't wash them until you're going to use them; the moisture could cause them to spoil while being stored.

Blueberries have been called one of the world's healthiest foods. They're very low in calories, contain no cholesterol and are a good source of fiber. One cup (250 mL) of berries provides about 25 percent of your daily recommended intake of vitamin C. Blueberries are also extremely rich in antioxidants, natural substances found in plants that are believed to help boost the immune system and aid in the prevention of heart disease, cancer and stroke.

EASY-ROLL GINGER COOKIES

preparation time	20 minutes
cooking time	15 minutes
makes	30 cookies

The key to these cookies is the soft and pliable dough, which makes them quick and easy to roll. It's difficult to eat just one of these pleasingly spicy and moist-in-the-middle cookies. It's best to have a stand mixer to make them (see Note).

ERIC'S OPTIONS
These make delicious ice cream sandwiches: simply put a scoop of vanilla ice cream between 2 ginger cookies, press together and freeze until the ice cream is solid again. To store, wrap the sandwich in plastic wrap and keep frozen until you're ready to serve them.

1¾ cups	all-purpose flour	425 mL
¾ tsp	baking soda	4 mL
2 tsp	ground ginger	10 mL
pinch	ground cloves	pinch
⅓ cup	butter, at room temperature	75 mL
1 cup	granulated sugar	250 mL
1	large egg	1
1 tsp	white vinegar	5 mL
¼ cup	molasses	60 mL

Place an oven rack in the middle position. Preheat the oven to 325°F (160°C). Line 2 large baking sheets with parchment paper.

Place the flour, baking soda, ginger and cloves in a bowl and whisk to combine. Place the butter and sugar in the bowl of your stand mixer and beat until light and well combined, about 3–4 minutes. Beat in the egg, vinegar and molasses. Add the flour mixture and beat until just combined.

Roll the dough into 1-inch (2.5 cm) balls and place on the baking sheets, spacing them about 2 inches (5 cm) apart. Bake, 1 sheet at a time, for 15 minutes. Cool on a rack, then store in an airtight container at room temperature for up to 2 weeks.

NOTE

If you don't have a stand mixer, you could vigorously beat the cookie dough with a large wooden spoon. Hand-held electric mixers don't work well with this batter; the beaters are too closely spaced and don't do a good job of pulling the dough together into a soft and pliable form.

TIPS FOR MAKING COOKIES

Invest in good-quality baking sheets that promote even baking. Baking sheets—also called cookie sheets—come in a variety of sizes, but buy larger ones so your cookies will have ample room to spread as they bake. The ones used when creating the recipes for this book were 13 x 18 inches (33 x 45 cm). For easy cleanup, line the sheets with parchment paper.

Read the recipe and make sure you have everything required. You don't want to be driving to the store for a missing ingredient while the unbaked batter languishes on your countertop.

Measure the ingredients carefully, using standard measuring spoons and cups and making sure your measurements are level, not heaped or almost full. Baking recipes are formulas, and if you're too far off the mark when measuring, you could end up with cookies that are flat and thin instead of puffed and plump, for instance.

Chill butter-rich cookies in the refrigerator for 20–30 minutes before baking. If you bake them right after rolling, the room-temperature butter, warmed even more during shaping, can melt and seep out of the cookies before the flour and other ingredients get a chance to set.

Bake cookies in the middle of the oven. If the rack is in the lower part of the oven they may burn on the bottom before they're baked. If it's in the upper half, the tops of the cookies may become overly brown before the cookie is baked through.

WHOLE WHEAT CHOCOLATE CHIP COOKIES

preparation time	20 minutes
cooking time	15 minutes
makes	20–24 cookies

Whole wheat flour adds fiber to this version of one of the world's favorite cookies.

ERIC'S OPTIONS
If you like nuts, replace ½ cup (125 mL) of the chocolate chips with ½ cup (125 mL) of chopped walnuts or pecans.

1¼ cups	whole wheat flour	310 mL
½ tsp	baking soda	2 mL
1½ cups	chocolate chips	375 mL
½ cup	butter, at room temperature	125 mL
¾ cup	packed golden brown sugar	175 mL
1 tsp	pure vanilla extract	5 mL
2	large eggs	2

Place an oven rack in the middle position. Preheat the oven to 325°F (160°C). Line 2 large baking sheets with parchment paper.

Place the flour and baking soda in a bowl and whisk to combine; stir in the chocolate chips. In another bowl, beat the butter, brown sugar and vanilla until well combined and lightened, about 3–4 minutes. Beat in the eggs, 1 at a time. Add the flour mixture and mix until just combined.

Drop 2 Tbsp (30 mL) amounts of the dough on the baking sheets, spacing them about 3 inches (8 cm) apart. Bake the cookies, 1 sheet at a time, for 15 minutes, or until golden brown. Cool on a rack, then store in an airtight container at room temperature for up to 2 weeks.

PEANUT BUTTER COOKIES

preparation time	·	20 minutes
cooking time	·	13–15 minutes
makes	·	24 cookies

Kids love to help make these cookies.

ERIC'S OPTIONS
Make peanut butter chocolate chip cookies by mixing ¾ cup (175 mL) of chocolate chips into the batter before rolling.

1¼ cups	all-purpose flour	310 mL
¾ tsp	baking soda	4 mL
½ tsp	baking powder	2 mL
¼ tsp	salt	1 mL
½ cup	granulated sugar	125 mL
½ cup	packed golden brown sugar	125 mL
½ cup	peanut butter	125 mL
¼ cup	vegetable shortening	60 mL
¼ cup	butter, at room temperature	60 mL
1	large egg	1

Line 2 large baking sheets with parchment paper. Whisk the flour, baking soda, baking powder and salt together in a bowl. Place the granulated sugar, brown sugar, peanut butter, shortening, butter and egg in a large bowl and beat until well combined. Add the flour mixture to the peanut butter mixture and beat until well combined.

Lightly flour your hands and roll the dough into 1½-inch (4 cm) balls. Place on the baking sheets, spacing them about 3 inches (8 cm) apart. Slightly flatten the cookies with a floured fork. Chill the cookies in the refrigerator for 30 minutes.

Place an oven rack in the middle position. Preheat the oven to 375°F (190°C). Bake the cookies, 1 tray at a time, for 13–15 minutes, until light golden brown. Cool on a rack, then store in an airtight container at room temperature for up to 2 weeks.

INDEX

"No cookbooks in my collection are more dogeared than *Everyone Can Cook* and *Everyone Can Cook Seafood*. Thank you, Eric, for dishing up this brilliant new volume of appetizers and tantalizing our taste buds once again!"

ELIZABETH LEVINSON, AWARD-WINNING AUTHOR AND COLUMNIST FOR *FOCUS* MAGAZINE

"The real joy of food is sharing. In his latest book, Eric continues his tradition of sharing creative, elegant and real food recipes. I predict many happy parties and family gatherings will be fuelled by this delicious book."

BILL JONES, CHEF, AUTHOR, AND FOOD CONSULTANT

"From casual to formal, Eric Akis takes the stress out of entertaining with this delectable new collection of easy recipes that really work."

CYNTHIA DAVID, CONTRIBUTING WRITER, *FOOD & DRINK* MAGAZINE

"Let the parties begin. Eric's new book is an exciting collection of approachable, easy-to-prepare appetizers, with great serving ideas. I can't wait for the next request to come my way ... Oh, just bring an appetizer!"

GAIL NORTON, CO-OWNER, THE COOKBOOK CO. AND PUBLISHER OF CALGARY'S *CITY PALATE* MAGAZINE

ERIC AKIS

EVERYONE**CAN**COOK
appetizers

over 100 tasty bites

ISBN 978-1-55285-793-9

"Eric's creative and straightforward recipes make me want to invite friends over for seafood—tonight!"
RON EADE, FOOD EDITOR, *OTTAWA CITIZEN*

"This book is a celebration of our oceans' bounty, well researched and beautifully executed. Eric Akis is a home cook who knows how to write a recipe the way home cooks like. They are uncomplicated, easy to understand, and make the main ingredient (seafood) the star. Bravo Eric!"
KARL WELLS, FOOD CHAIN, CBC COUNTRY CANADA CHANNEL

"It's odd that a definitive Canadian seafood book has not been written before now, given that the country has the longest coastline of earth. Well, the wait is over…this is IT!"
ANITA STEWART, AUTHOR AND CULINARY ACTIVIST

"Eric teaches us how to jump right in when it comes to cooking seafood. He makes cooking seafood easy. But most important, the recipes are reliable and always turn out."
CAROLYN HEIMAN, FEATURES EDITOR, *VICTORIA TIMES COLONIST*

"So, you love seafood and order it all the time when you're out. But at home you're not so sure about how to choose and cook fish. Eric Akis has the answers, with buying tips and tempting recipes that run the range from Tuesday supper to special occasions. Enjoying seafood has never been more inviting— or approachable."
ELIZABETH BAIRD, FOOD AND NUTRITION EDITOR, *CANADIAN LIVING MAGAZINE*

EVERYONECANCOOK
seafood

ERIC AKIS

ISBN 978-1-55285-614-7

"This collection of lively, user-friendly recipes makes me want to start cooking at once."
JULIAN ARMSTRONG, FOOD EDITOR, *THE GAZETTE* (MONTREAL)

"Eric is a lively, talented food writer who gives our readers recipes that are easily made—and are simply delicious."
BARB WILKINSON, FEATURES EDITOR, *EDMONTON JOURNAL*

"Our readers look to Eric for dependable recipes that have flair and he delivers every time."
CAROLYN HEIMAN, FEATURES EDITOR, *VICTORIA TIMES COLONIST*

"Eric Akis is a fine chef who understands simplicity and finesse in cooking. His book is modern home cooking, with easy-to-make recipes that are honest, free-wheeling, and mouth-watering. It is the perfect kitchen companion. Keep it by your stove and refer to it often!"
GARY HYNES, EDITOR, *EAT MAGAZINE*

"I will be reaching for *Everyone Can Cook* just as I reach for my favourite cooking pot. Now I can throw away my tattered collection of Eric's columns. It is user friendly and the results are delicious—the perfect combination."
NOEL RICHARDSON, BESTSELLING FOOD WRITER AND CO-OWNER OF RAVENHILL FARM

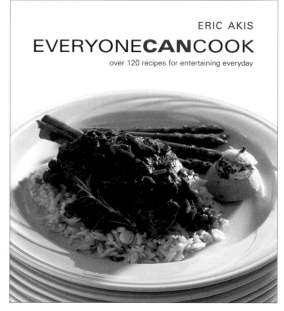

ERIC AKIS

EVERYONE**CAN**COOK

over 120 recipes for entertaining everyday

ISBN 978-1-55285-448-8

ABOUT
THE AUTHOR

Eric Akis is in his 12th year as food writer for the *Victoria Times Colonist.* His twice-weekly food features also appear in a variety of other newspapers across Canada. Prior to becoming a journalist, Akis worked for 15 years as a chef in a variety of operations. He is the author of the best-selling cookbooks *Everyone Can Cook, Everyone Can Cook Seafood* and *Everyone Can Cook Appetizers.* When not writing, Akis works as a food consultant, providing services such as food styling and recipe and product development. His clients include Thrifty Foods, a highly regarded West Coast supermarket chain. Akis lives in Victoria, BC, with his wife, Cheryl Warwick (also a chef), and teenage son, Tyler.